HOW

Cookery, Italian
Futurism: cookery
Futurism (Art)

the
futurist
cookbook

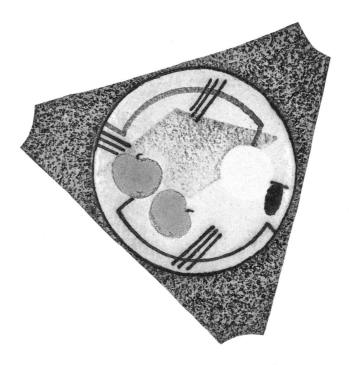

Previous page: Dish designed by Marinetti and executed by Giuseppe Mazzotti.

Facing page: Marinetti in a photograph by Greco, La Spezia.

MARINETTI

the futurist cookbook

Translated by Suzanne Brill
Edited with an introduction by Lesley Chamberlain
Trefoil Publications, London
Bedford Arts, Publishers, San Francisco

Published in UK by Trefoil Publications Ltd
Published in USA by Bedford Arts
First published 1989
Copyright © 1989 by © Estate of F.T. Marinetti
English translation © Suzanne Brill, 1989
Introduction © Lesley Chamberlain, 1989
Illustrations and reproductions © Luce Marinetti, 1989
          ISBN 0 86294 140 7 (UK) cloth
Library of Congress Cataloging-in-Publication Data
Marinetti, Filippo Tommaso, 1876-1944.
        The futurist cookbook.
        Translation of: La cucina futurista.
        1. Cookery, Italian. 2. Futurism (Art).
        3. Gastronomy. I. Title.
TX723.M32913   1989   641.5945   89 – 17705
ISBN 0-938491-30-X
ISBN 0-938491-31-8 (pbk.)
Typeset in Bodoni and Helvetica by OTS (Typesetting) Limited to a design
by Elizabeth van Amerongen
Cover design by Conway Lloyd Morgan and Liz McQuiston
Printed by The Amadeus Press

contents

translator's acknowledgements

I would like to thank Claire Clifton for suggesting the project to me in the first place and for help with culinary terms, Anna Maria Franceschelli for assistance with ambiguities of language and Norma Turner for versifying in english Folgore's *dazzling appetizer*. Thanks also go to Lutz Becker, Luce Marinetti and Professor Allessandro Vaciago, director of the Italian Institute, London, and his family.

Suzanne Brill.

Set of dishes for a 'Life of Marinetti' cycle

introduction

In 1932 the Italian Futurist Filippo Tommaso Marinetti proposed a revolution in food. He dined his way from Milan to Paris to Budapest, staging eye-catching talks to back his campaign, and newspapers caught on to him.

ITALIANS MAY DOWN SPAGHETTI!

This story in the *Chicago Tribune* took hold of a prominent aspect of Futurist food. *THE FUTURIST COOKBOOK* contained a manifesto to revitalize Italian culture by changing the way Italians ate — Marinetti found them sluggish and lacking in energy and originality.

But so much for the newspapers. Marinetti had broader aims. They omitted to say his 'cookbook' was one of the best artistic jokes of the century.

The Futurist Cookbook was designed to wrench food out of the nineteenth-century 'bourgeois' past and bring it into the dynamic, technological, urban twentieth century. Marinetti wrote forcefully and excitedly; his iconoclastic energy, his poetic inventiveness and vigorous physical presence filled every page. *The Futurist Cookbook* was a serious joke, revolutionary in the first instance because it overturned with ribald laughter everything 'food' and 'cookbooks' held sacred: the family table, great 'recipes', established notions of goodness and taste. Envisage the nineteenth-century culinary ideal — a Romantic, Rousseauan notion — as one of nourishing fare, gathered from the countryside and prepared at length with loving care. Marinetti blasted this pastoral food from the landscape and with modern brashness flew in a low-calorie, high-tech cuisine. Wasn't that better suited to life in the fast-moving city? he asked but didn't wait to hear the answer, immediately writing instead his version of a 'cookbook': one in which food scenarios, food tableaux and food sculptures had annihilated traditional kitchen instructions.

Futurist 'cooking' was revolutionary and a joke because actually it was about food as raw material for art. It was not a collection of recipes for self-nourishment but a disguised artistic game, full of ideas for avant-garde experiments. Spinach, tomato, egg whites and prunes: you name the ingredient. Marinetti looked upon them all as colours and building blocks and put them together with colour and shape and ideas in mind, not taste.

Thirdly, *The Futurist Cookbook* was a lusty work, circling exuberantly round the table and the bed. It was more than the traditional reader dared expect of a food manual, this textbook of expanded sensual appreciation. It was and remains a book to be re-created and enjoyed each time it is read, a book which is liberating in its enthusiasm.

Historically, *The Futurist Cookbook* is a late manifestation of Italian Futurism, a passionate and highly influential movement in art at the beginning of the century. When Marinetti published the first and most famous of his Futurist manifestoes in February 1909 it marked a definitive moment in the shift from nineteenth-century Romanticism to a twentieth-century passion for speed and technology. Indeed without Futurism the avant-garde movements of subsequent decades are hardly conceivable. Futurist manifestoes by Marinetti and others appeared annually until 1916, interrupted by the First World War, and continued spasmodically afterwards. What prompted Futurism were radical innovations in physics, technology, painting and music; also an uneasy political atmosphere which was soon to erupt in global conflict and national revolution. The Italian Futurists strove to liberate language, art and life from tradition and convention. They found their models and their tools in those extraordinary phenomena of the new age: the motor car and the aeroplane, the cinema and the telephone. The inspiration was brilliant and the tone merciless. Marinetti – in a violent, lyrical voice still just as strident 20 years later – wrote of his desire to trample on anything *passéist*. He exalted the dynamic present and future. This is a typical extract from the 1909 manifesto:

> We stand on the last promontory of the centuries!
>
> We will glorify war – the world's only hygiene – militarism, patriotism, the destructive gesture of freedom-bringers, beautiful ideas worth dying for, and scorn for women.
>
> We will destroy the museums, libraries, academies of every kind, will fight moralism, feminism, every opportunistic or utilitarian cowardice.
>
> We will sing of great crowds excited by work, by pleasure, and by riot; we will sing of the multi-coloured, polyphonic tides of revolution in the modern capitals; we will sing of the vibrant nightly fervour of arsenals and shipyards blazing with violent electric moons; greedy railway stations that devour smoke-plumed serpents; factories hung on

clouds by the crooked lines of their smoke; bridges that stride the rivers like giant gymnasts, flashing in the sun with a glitter of knives; adventurous steamers that sniff the horizon; deep-chested locomotives whose wheels paw the tracks like the hooves of enormous steel horses bridled by tubing; and the sleek flight of planes whose propellers chatter in the wind like banners and seem to cheer like an enthusiastic crowd.

It is from Italy that we launch through the world this violently upsetting incendiary manifesto of ours. With it, today, we establish *Futurism*, because we want to free this land from its smelly gangrene of professors, archaeologists, *ciceroni* and antiquarians. For too long Italy has been a dealer in second-hand clothes. We mean to free her from the numberless museums that cover her like so many graveyards...

As this extract shows, Marinetti's Futurism was both an artistic and a nationalistic movement, sometimes subtle, sometimes crude. Marinetti could create breathtaking imagery one moment, and be happy to tub-thump the next. He was at his best as a visual poet/sculptor/painter in words and at his most offensive and tedious as a publicist. Those same talents and deficiencies went into *The Futurist Cookbook*.

They are what makes Marinetti's achievement so controversial. As a poet he wanted to breathe new life into the language; as a patriot he desired the re-invigoration of the country's stultified cultural forces. The odd thing was that he dealt with subtle aesthetic and mass political issues in the same way. His impulse to deal in one breath with, say, poetry, transport, hotels and sculpture, is indeed why Futurism, with its far-reaching scope and effects, can be called the first mass art movement of the twentieth century. Intending to transform not only poetry and sculpture but all daily experience, from toys and clothes to politics and social behaviour, it was sweeping and totalitarian in spirit.

Futurism was devoted to novelty and shock. All the Futurist art forms espoused the unexpected and disharmonious and generally Futurism addressed itself to the public in immoderate terms. The racism, violence and misogyny of *The Futurist Cookbook* are typical of the movement's excesses. In everyday life Futurism meant mass meetings, manifestoes in newspapers, or even a blow on the head. Marinetti was not averse to using his fists as the real-life complement to the manifesto form in art. Indeed it meant everything to Futurism that art and life were no longer separate. The Futurists believed – and they at times described their views as a religion – that all human experience was liberated by the availability of art in everyday life, the synthesis of *arte-vita*. It was

The wreck of Marinetti's car after an accident in 1909, an incident referred to in the first Futurist Manifesto.

A number of Futurist manifestoes

Marinetti, 1927

PRAMPOLINI, Rome

*Detail from Enrico Prampolini's
cover for the Futurist 'Aristocracy'
magazine, edited by Nanni Leone
Castelli, New York 1923.*

11

a kind of romanticism about the humanizing possibilities of technology. They chose the accessible form of the manifesto – or borrowed it from revolutionary politics – to spread their message, backed up by the publicity tour. Marinetti, a powerful public speaker and a wily journalist, was master of both these popular forms of communication. But the means didn't detract from the aesthetic seriousness of the campaign. It was a highbrow matter, to try to raise the artistic consciousness of the nation *en masse*. It led amongst other things to the unique joke of *The Futurist Cookbook*. No other cultural movement has produced a provocative work about art disguised as easy-to-read cookbook. The book, like the movement, owes its essence to the contradictory genius of Marinetti.

The Cookbook belongs to what has since been termed the second wave of Futurism. A combination of accidents, battle-losses and mutual disaffection among the leading personalities had ended the first wave around the time of the Great War. By 1917 the painter Umberto Boccioni and the architect Antonio Sant'Elia were dead, while the painter Carlo Carrà had abandoned his Futurist style. Undaunted Marinetti founded a so-called Second Futurism, with new followers and publications and new applications for Futurist ideas. It lasted until the outbreak of the Second World War.

The Futurist Cookbook was written with the painter Luigi Colombo Fillìa, who like the majority of the second-wave Futurists was not an artist of the first rank. The renewed movement however attracted more than a hundred painters as well as poets, sculptors and musicians, all of them dedicated to the pursuit of new sensations and the representation of speed and simultaneity. The talented painter Giacomo Balla, the painter, engraver and outstanding stage designer Fortunato Depero and the architect and designer Enrico Prampolini, all of whom play their part in *The Futurist Cookbook*, led the crowded field. The second-wave Futurists' interests developed particularly as air travel and radio became more and more part of daily life. In 1929 Marinetti published *The Manifesto of Aeropainting* and with Fedele Azari *The First Aerodictionary*, which put on record the Futurists' fascination with light and speed and colour and perspective from the air. The group of nine who signed the 1929 manifesto: Marinetti's wife Benedetta, Depero, Balla, Dottori, Fillìa, Marinetti, Prampolini, Somenzi and Tato, henceforth referred to themselves as Futurist aeropainters, aerosculptors and aeropoets. The aerofuturists took up the earlier generation's interest in sounds, noises and smells, and Marinetti pursued a fascination with touch. *The Futurist Cookbook* experiments with radio, telephone and gramophone and contains a hilarious pyjama-clad adventure into tactilism.

Futurist ideas were eye-catching, stimulating, wide-ranging and shocking, but always the personality of Marinetti was of supreme importance. He was born the second son of a lawyer, Enrico Marinetti, in 1876 in Alexandria, Egypt. He had a Jesuit education in French and while he was still at the Saint Francis Xavier College from 1892-94 he published a literary magazine. It is not clear for what reason he was later expelled — perhaps for introducing the novels of Émile Zola to the school — but he finished his schooling in Paris then studied law at the universities of Pavia and Genoa. Meanwhile his father, having amassed substantial wealth in Egypt, moved the family to Milan. Marinetti perhaps considered a legal career, but did not cease contributing to literary magazines and writing poetry. He published his first work in the fashionable free verse style in 1898 and devoted himself entirely to Italian and French literature from 1900. As he emerged as an artist with a passion to find a new poetic language his mentors were above all the French Symbolist poets: Hugo, Baudelaire, Mallarmé, Rimbaud and Verlaine.

Marinetti's Futurism is not difficult to distill from his family and intellectual origins. His passion for all that seemed anti-bourgeois was an essential artistic attitude of the poetry in which he had steeped himself, though it may also have been a reaction against his early strict schooling. His love of machines could also find its roots in Baudelaire's depiction of the evil of the city, though Marinetti was always an optimist. For his Futurism essentially he transferred romantic energy away from the symbols of nature — so attractive to past poets — towards technology, the god of the future. Then he looked to the new art to fuel and strengthen his social philosophy. The symbolism of high-speed technology suggested new weapons with which to attack the unchanging comfortable torpor of the establishment, whether literary, social or culinary. The main point about Marinetti's outlook is that his mind moved very freely between art and life, never stopping to distinguish between the symbolic and the real.

It was a weakness and a source of confusion. For all his transparency, his energy and his optimism Marinetti has passed into history surrounded by

Marinetti fighting a duel with the journalist Carlo Chiminelli in Rome, 30th April 1924: he was wounded.

obloquy, well-known for his violent style of writing and his fondness for real violence. It is remembered that he issued a Futurist manifesto glorifying war, that he revelled in his military experiences (times often evoked in *The Futurist Cookbook*) and that he volunteered for the front even in middle age. The question of his violence remains vexed.

Few readers of the Dynamic Dinner in *La Cucina* will fail to find offensive its brutal 'murder' of the quiet doctor who only wishes to eat his meal in peace. No one who has seen Marinetti's consistently arrogant pose in photographs — as if he were defending himself against the new medium — will think of him as a gentle man. Yet we have the testament of his family that he was a devoted husband and father to his four children and of those close to him that he was a generous friend. Against the photographs too there is Carrà's intense and lyrical cubist portrait of Marinetti, which perhaps suggests that the transition from romantic to Futurist was by way of a pose: a way of

The Marinetti family, photographed by Luxardo, 1936: from the left, his daughter Ala, his wife Benedetta and daughters Vittoria and Luce.

confronting the twentieth century, and its mass media and public, with a sustained artistic performance of 'life'.

At the height of Futurism Marinetti became embroiled with Mussolini and Fascism, a connection which led to his being ignored by the Italian public for three decades after the war. His Fascism remains a hotly-debated question, again one not helped by Marinetti's constant interweaving of art and life. A belief in violent action together with a passionate commitment to the renewal of Italy as a powerful nation involved him in illegal demonstrations for several years from 1915, when he was arrested twice in three months, the second time with other Futurists and Mussolini. Service in the armed forces – during which time he was awarded a medal for bravery in the successful battle of Vittorio Veneto – temporarily diverted his energies but only until the end of 1918, when Futurist-Fascist political groups were formed in various Italian cities. Indeed the following year was a nadir. Throughout 1919 Marinetti lent

F.T. Marinetti in the uniform of the Italian Academy, of which he was a founder member.

his skills as an orator to the young Fascist cause. He also took part, for the only time in his life, in the first Fascist activist success, which ended in the destruction of the office and printing works of the socialist newspaper *Avanti!* in Milan. Moreover it was this action by *arditi* — ex-servicemen who had banded together against socialism — which actually taught Mussolini that armed intimidation was a useful political tactic against the opposition. By May 1920 however Marinetti was accusing even the Fascists of being reactionary and *passéist* and he resigned from the Party. There was a rapprochement in 1923-24 but, now married, he never became so deeply engaged again. It was true in 1926 Mussolini personally selected him as a founder member of his nationalistic Italian Academy. But Marinetti's original, energetic personality and the vitality and intellectual spark of Futurism never fitted with the Duce's abysmal artistic ideal — of something close to Soviet socialist realism. In 1938 Marinetti also strongly condemned anti-semitism in Fascist politics and art. Nevertheless he never ceased to fight in body and spirit for a vibrant, original Italy.

He was 55 when he joined Italian troops in Russia in 1942, only to return exhausted to Venice the following year. In August 1944 he transferred his family to the region of Lake Como, where with Italian defeat in prospect they would be close to the border with neutral Switzerland. It was a plan many of the Fascist hierarchy, not excluding Mussolini himself, had in mind. But at Bellagio, a small town on the lake, Marinetti died of a heart attack on December 2, 1944.

The Futurist Cookbook certainly expressed Fascist ideals in 1932. How far may be seen in the section entitled Against Xenomania. Marinetti calls for undiluted independence in social and artistic activity to put Italy back on the cultural map. The goal in terms of Italian civilisation is greater than anything Fascism dreamed of, but the intolerant tone, culminating in Marinetti's final undertaking, in a moment of military reminiscence, to shoot xenomanes on sight, was hardly superior. Like Mussolini, Marinetti also wished to make Italian vocabulary more patriotic. The glossary to *The Futurist Cookbook* suggested replacing foreign words such as 'menu' and 'sandwich' and 'consommé' with Futurist neologisms. Mussolini had banned similar foreign terms like 'il weekend'.

But Marinetti, with his radical distaste for discipline, hierarchy and tradition in culture, remained the poet: the anarchist whose ideals could never have served the Fascist purpose for longer than a passing hour. His talent was too individual and too riotous. He could invent a pro-Italian vocabulary for the Futurist Cookbook, but he could not unlearn French nor put aside his linguistic jokes. He made a characteristic one in listing the dishes for the First Futurist Banquet in Turin. 'Oca grassa' was served. Mentally translated into French this was 'oie grasse', a pun on 'foie gras'.

The Futurist Cookbook is a densely poetic text woven around repeated concepts and images. Some of the concepts are explained in Marinetti's glossary, and tactilism is self-evident. Of the others, belonging to the first stage of Futurism, the Words-in-Liberty was an ideal of free association — a kind of writing without punctuation and syntax — first proclaimed in 1913, with the aim of freeing words from stale contexts and allowing 'absolute freedom of images and analogies'. To it *The Futurist Cookbook* owes its frequent undivided strings of adjectives and substantives. The other prominent idea is simultaneity. This was well described in a manifesto by Boccioni in 1914 as ' a lyrical exaltation, a plastic manifestation of a new absolute, speed; a new and marvellous spectacle, modern life; a new fever, scientific discovery. Simultaneity is a condition in which the various elements which constitute dynamism are present... It is the lyrical manifestation of modern ways of looking at life, based on speed and contemporaneity in knowledge and communication ...'

Marinetti's idealized love of Africa, reflected in all his literary writings and poetry, runs through *The Futurist Cookbook* like a *leitmotif*. Egypt was his birthplace, then in 1911 he went to Libya as a war correspondent; he also took a great interest in the former Italian colonies of Ethiopia and Somalia. Africa served Futurism particularly well because it was rich source of surprises, shocks and unknown elements. In *The Futurist Cookbook*, describing The Great Futurist Banquet in Paris, Marinetti writes of '... an atmosphere simultaneously African and mechanical ... a splendid rendering of the wish to interpret colonial motifs according to a modern and Futurist sensibility'. The exotic continent is reflected in the names of Futurist dishes, in Marinetti's fascination with Negroes (the acceptable word in his day) and in his deliberately unusual choice of ingredients.

The Futurist Cookbook is an extraordinary and unique book. It is funny, almost slapstick in its attacks on bourgeois habits, stuffy professors and the war between the sexes. At eating times it has the atmosphere of a children's party. Overall

Marinetti at home with his daughters, Vittoria (the eldest) and Ala, 1932. The decorative vase and table are from his family's home in Alexandria, Egypt.

the form is a collage containing many different messages and textures, including newspaper quotes, personal letters, true reportage, and spoof history. It talks about food in ways which are lessons in modern painting and staging. Each 'formula' is an experiment in representation, the picture only revealing itself on completion. The results include a ski trip, a Fascist uniform, a woman's breasts, coitus, a tennis game and an unflushed lavatory bowl. Meanwhile The Provocative and Definitive Futurist Banquets are so rich in visual imagery they can be called food charades or scenarios; they are sumptuous three-dimensional pictures; short wordless poetic films; and the literary achievement in these charades – perhaps here it would be more appropriate to call them prose-poems – often equals that of the spectacular opening parable. It is a book with a powerful atmosphere, redounding with the contradictions of Marinetti's personality. For an anti-bourgeois he is addicted to pomp and official titles and frequently refers to himself as 'His Excellency' and 'Academician'. He hates speeches except when he is speaking. He grabs attention, wants applause and loves playing practical jokes.

Historically *The Futurist Cookbook* had a single function as a cookery book: it explicitly challenged all that was established by Pelegrino Artusi in *L'Arte di mangiar bene*, the summit of nineteenth-century family cooking. I have to confess though that the first time I approached Marinetti's work I took it for a cookbook. It was only when I made some of the food that I began to see its poetic appeal. Food is the medium for an eccentric paean to sensual freedom, optimism and childlike, amoral innocence. In that respect so far as I know *The Futurist Cookbook* has only once been answered, by Aldous Huxley's *Brave New World*.

The text is based on the one as printed by Sonzogno in 1932, but excluding a section of the original repeated in French and a selection of international quotations on the value of Futurism. We have left Marinetti's replacements for foreign words in Italian, together with his occasional inconsistencies in usage, spelling and punctuation. His many patriotic references to Italian products, including Tuscan vinsanto, white wines from the villages of Albana and Gavi, Fernet bitters, the 'Ricasoli' brand of Chianti, 'Cirio' brand preserves, Sienese panforte spice cake and various Italian liqueurs and spirits – Aurum, Strega, Rosolio, Grappa among them – have also been left untranslated.

Lesley Chamberlain
London August 1989

Contrary to criticisms already launched and those fore-seeable, the Futurist culinary revolution described in this book has the lofty, noble and universally expedient aim of changing radically the eating habits of our race, strengthening it, dynamizing it and spiritualizing it with brand-new food combinations in which experiment, intelligence and imagination will economically take the place of quantity, banality, repetition and expense.

This Futurist cooking of ours, tuned to high speeds like the motor of a hydroplane, will seem to some trembling traditionalists both mad and dangerous: but its ultimate aim, is to create a harmony between man's palate and his life today and tomorrow.

Apart from celebrated and legendary exceptions, until now men have fed themselves like ants, rats, cats or oxen. Now with the Futurists the first human way of eating is born. We mean the art of self-nourishment. Like all the arts, it eschews plagiarism and demands creative originality.

It is not by chance this work is published during a world economic crisis, which has clearly inspired a dangerous depressing panic, though its future direction remains unclear. We propose as an antidote to this panic a Futurist way of cooking, that is: optimism at the table.

A detail from the programme cover by Prampolini of the Futurist Pantomime at the Madeleine Theatre, Paris, 1927.

the dinner that stopped a suicide

On May 11th 1930 the poet Marinetti left for Lake Trasimeno by car in response to this strange, mysterious and unnerving telegram:

"Dearest friend since She departed forever have been wracked with tormenting anguish Stop immense sadness prevents my survival Stop beg you come immediately before arrival of the one who resembles her too much but not enough GIULIO."

Determined to save his friend, Marinetti had by telephone entreated the help of Prampolini and Fillìa, whose great genius as Aeropainters seemed to him made for such an undoubtedly grave situation.

With the precision of a surgeon the car driver sought and found the villa, among the putrid banks and heaving reed beds of the lake. In reality, hidden at the end of the park, between umbrella pines offering themselves up to Paradise and cypress trees diabolically infused with the ink of the Inferno, stood a veritable Royal Palace, not just a villa. On the doorstep, at the car door, the emaciated face and far too white hand of Giulio Onesti. This pseudonym, which masked his real name, and his combative and creative participation in the Futurist evenings of twenty years ago, his life of science and wealth accumulated at the Cape of Good Hope, and his sudden flight from inhabited places, filled the liberated conversation which preceded dinner in the polychrome quisibeve of the villa.

At the table, in a room hung with the red velvet of remorse and absorbing through its wide windows the light of a newborn half-moon rising but already immersed in death in the waters of the lake, Giulio murmured:

'I sense your palates are bored with antiquated ways and I feel your belief that to eat like this is to prepare for suicide. You're my old friends and I'm going to speak plainly: for the past three days the idea of suicide has filled this whole house and the park too. But so far I have not yet had the strength to cross the threshold. What do you advise?'

A long silence.

'Would you like to know why? I'll tell you. She — you know her, Marinetti! — She met her death three days ago in New York. I'm sure she's calling me. But by a strange coincidence a new and significant fact has intervened. Yesterday I received this message. It's from the other one, who resembles her ... too much ... but not enough. Another time I'll tell you her name and who she is. She announces her imminent arrival ...'

A long silence. Then Giulio was overcome with irrepressible, convulsive shivering.

'I will not, I must not betray death. I'll kill myself tonight.'

'Unless?' cried Prampolini.

'Unless?' repeated Fillìa.

'Unless?' concluded Marinetti, 'unless you take us instantly to your splendid, well-stocked kitchens.'

With the cooks terrified, having been dictatorially deprived of their authority, and the fires lit, Enrico Prampolini cried: 'Our ingenious hands need a hundred sacks of the following indispensable ingredients: chestnut flour, wheat flour, ground almonds, rye flour, cornmeal, cocoa powder, red pepper, sugar and eggs. Ten jars of honey, oil and milk. A quintal of dates and bananas.'

'It will be done this very night,' commanded Giulio.

The servants immediately began to fetch great heavy sacks, emptying them into pyramidal heaps of yellow, white, black and red and transforming the kitchens into fantastic laboratories where enormous upturned saucepans on the floor changed into grandiose pedestals predisposed to supporting unpredictable statuary.

'To work, my aeropainters and aerosculptors!' said Marinetti. 'My aeropoetry will ventilate your brains like whirring propellers.'

Fillìa improvised a sculptured aerocomplex of chestnut flour, eggs, milk and cocoa in which planes of nocturnal atmosphere were intersected by planes of greyish dawn, with expressive spirals of wind piped in pastry.

Enrico Prampolini, who had jealously surrounded his creative work with screens, cried out as the first light from the lucent horizon filtered through the open window:

'At last I hold her in my arms and she is beautiful, fascinating, carnal enough to cure any suicidal desire. Come and admire her!'

The screens vanished and there appeared the mysterious soft trembling sculptured complex which was her. Edible. In fact the flesh of the curve signifying the synthesis of every movement of her hips was even appetizing. And she shone with a sugary down peculiar to her which excited the very enamel on the teeth in the attentive mouths of his two companions. Higher up, the spherical sweetnesses of all ideal breasts spoke from a geometric distance to the dome of the stomach, supported by the force-lines of dynamic thighs.

'Don't come near!' He cried to Marinetti and Fillìa. 'Don't smell her. Go away. You have evil, voracious mouths. You would eat her away from me without stopping for breath.'

They set to work again, deliciously stimulated by the long elastic rays of sunrise, the rosy clouds, and the trilling of birds and the creaking of wood in waters whose green lacquer cracked in flashes of scintillating gold.

Intoxicating atmosphere lavish in forms and colours with sharp planes of light and smooth round splendours which high up the droning of an aeroplane was shaping into melody.

Inspired hands. Flared nostrils to guide teeth and fingernails. At seven The Passion of the Blondes rose from the largest oven in the kitchen, another tall sculptured complex of puff pastry modelled in descending pyramidal planes, each one of which had a slight curvature peculiar to a mouth, a stomach or a thigh, its own way of fluttering sensually, its own smile on its lips. On top a cylinder made from Indian corn turned on an axis and as it rotated faster and faster it flung out into the room an enormous mass of golden spun sugar.

Designed by Marinetti and constructed under his direction by Giulio Onesti, unexpectedly turned sculptor-cook, anxious and trembling, the sculpture was placed by him on the upturned bottom of a gigantic copper saucepan.

Instantly it so rivalled the sun's rays in brilliance that its intoxicated maker tongue-kissed his work like a child.

Then Prampolini and Fillìa unmoulded their work: High Speed, a swirling lasso of pastry, synthesis of every car's longing for curves in the distance, and Lightness of Flight which offered the watching mouths 29 silvered lady's ankles mixed with wheel hubs and propeller blades, all made of soft leavened dough.

With the mouths of friendly cannibals Giulio Onesti, Marinetti, Prampolini and Fillìa restored themselves with a tasty morsel of statue every now and again.

In the silence of the afternoon the muscular demands of the work accelerated. Masses of tasty bulk to be transported. The torrent of time swept beneath their feet as they perched uncertainly on the smooth, unstable pebbles of their thoughts.

During a pause Giulio Onesti said:

'Whether the New One arrives with the twilight or with the night we shall offer her an artistic edible truly unexpected sunrise. But it's not for her we shall work. Her mouth, ideal as it may be, will be that of any female guest.'

But Giulio Onesti displayed an uneasiness which did not correspond to the Futurist serenity of his brain. He feared what was to come. That imminent mouth also worried the three Futurists at work. They sensed it and savoured it among the flavours of vanilla, sponge biscuits, of roses violets and acacias; flavours which a Spring breeze, as intoxicated with sculpture as they were, was mixing together in the park and the kitchen.

Silence again.

Suddenly a sculptural complex of chocolate and nougat, representing the Forms of Nostalgia and of the Past collapsed with a crash, spattering everything with sticky dark liquid.

Calmly take up the material again. Crucify it with sharp nails of will. Nerves. Passion. Lip-felt joy. All of heaven in the nostrils. A smack of the tongue. Hold the breath so as not to blunt a chiselled flavour.

At six in the evening night had already thickened in two great emerald eyes which were taking shape above sweet dunes of flesh and sand. The masterpiece. It was entitled The Curves of the World and their Secrets. Marinetti, Prampolini and Fillìa, in collaboration, had inoculated it with the gentle magnetism of the most beautiful women and the most beautiful Africas ever dreamed of. Its sloping architecture of soft curves following one upon the other to heaven concealed the grace of the world's most feminine little feet in a thick and sugary network of green oasis-palms, whose tufts were mechanically interlocked by cog-wheels. Further down could be heard the happy chattering of Birds of Paradise. It was a motorized edible sculpture, perfect.

Prampolini said: 'You'll see, he'll win her.'

The bell at the park gate rang telepathically in the distance.

●

At midnight, in the vast armoury, the Futurists Marinetti, Prampolini and Fillìa awaited the master of the house, invited in his turn to inaugurate and taste the Great Exhibition of Edible Sculpture, at last ready.

In a corner, near an expanse of window glimmering with green and sickly sharp reflections from the lake, masses of halberds and bundles of rifles quarreling with two enormous mountain cannon had been piled up and swept aside as if by a magic superhuman force.

And truly superhuman was the Exhibition of 22 edible sculptures under 11 electric lightbulbs resplendent in the corner opposite.

Of them all, the one entitled The Curves of the World and Their Secrets was disturbing. As if sucked dry by so much lyrical-sculptural aerodynamism, the exhausted Marinetti, Prampolini and Fillìa lay on a huge Danish feather quilt which in the mother-of-pearl softness of the electric light seemed to be transporting itself, a cloud fixed in a car's headlamps.

But they jumped eagerly to their feet at the sound of two voices, one manly but tired, the other feminine and aggressive. A brief exchange of stupefying pleasantries to her, from her. Then the immobility and silence of the five.

A very beautiful woman, but of a traditional beauty. It was her good fortune that her large green eyes, full of false childish ingenuousness, under a low forehead drowned in a rich abundance of almost blonde and almost chestnut hair, revolutionized and ignited the tranquil curves and the exquisite elegance of every detail of her neck, shoulders and slim hips barely sheathed in gold moiré.

'Don't think I'm a fool,' she murmured with languid grace, 'I'm dazzled. Your genius frightens me! I beg you, explain the reasons, the intentions and thoughts that possessed you while you were sculpting all of these delicious smells flavours colours and forms.'

To her, as she cautiously and sculpturally burrowed in the cushions furs and rugs to make for her own body the nest-lair of a delicate wild beast, Marinetti, Prampolini and Fillìa spoke alternately, like three well-oiled pistons of the same machine.

Lying prone at their feet, with his face turned to the centre of the Earth, Giulio Onesti dreamed or listened.

They said:

'We love women. Often we have tortured ourselves with a thousand greedy kisses in our anxiety to eat one of them. Nudes seemed to us always tragically dressed. Their hearts, if clenched with the supreme pleasure of love, seemed to us the ideal fruit to bite to chew to suck. All of the forms of hunger that characterize love guided us in the creation of these works of genius and of insatiable tongues. They are our states of mind realized. The fascination, the childish grace, the ingenuousness, the dawn, the modesty, the furious whirl-pool of sex, the rain of all mad cravings and caprices, the itchings and rebel-lions against age-old bondage, one and all have found here, through the medium of our hands, an artistic expression so intense that it demands not only eyes and admiration, not only touch and caresses, but teeth, tongue, stomach, gut – all equally in love.'

'For pity's sake,' she smiled and sighed, 'you're like wild beasts. Control yourselves!'

'No one will eat you for the moment,' said Prampolini, 'unless the very thin Fillìa...'

Marinetti cut in:

'In this catalogue of the Exhibition of Edible Sculpture, you will be able to read tonight the original erotic-sentimental chatter which aroused in the artists certain seemingly incomprehensible flavours and forms. It is light, aerial art. Ephemeral art. Edible art. The fugitive eternal feminine imprisoned in the stomach. The painful, superacute tension of the most frenetic lusts finally grati-fied. You consider us wild; others think us highly complicated and civilized. We are the instinctive new elements of the great Machine future lyrical plastic architectonic, all new laws, all new instructions.'

A long period of silence struck down Marinetti, Prampolini and Fillìa with sleep. The woman contemplated them for a few moments, then threw back her head and slept too. The faint whistling of their breath, laden with desires, images and passions harmonized with the whistling and rustling of the reeds in the lake scraped by the night breeze.

A hundred violet-azure bluebottles launched an impassioned artistic assault on the electric bulbs high up, these incandescences also to be sculpted at any cost and as quickly as possible.

All at once Giulio, with the wary back of a thief, turned his head a fraction to right and left, making sure that the sculptors and sculptress of life were fast sleep. Springing lightly to his feet, without making a sound, he ran his eyes around his great armoury and then resolutely made for the towering sculpture of The Curves of the World and Their Secrets. Kneeling before it he began like a lover to adore it with his lips, tongue and teeth. Searching and overturning the pretty little sugar palm tree like a ravenous tiger, he bit off and ate a sweet little foot skating on a cloud.

At three that morning, with a terrible writhing of his loins, he bit into the dense heart-of-hearts of pleasure. Sculptors and sculptress slept. At dawn he devoured the mammellary spheres of all mothers' milk. When his tongue skimmed the long eyelashes that guarded the great jewels of her gaze, the clouds which had gathered swiftly over the lake suddenly loosed a violent orange thunderbolt whose long green rays tore through the reed beds a few metres from the armoury.

A flood of vain tears followed. Endless. It seemed only to deepen the sleep of the sculptors and sculptress of life.

Perhaps to refresh himself Giulio went out bare-headed into the park crisscrossed by the reverberating sounds of thunder. He felt at the same time unencumbered, liberated, empty and bursting. Enjoying and enjoyed. Possessor and possessed. Unique and complete.

Marinetti in Paris in the 1920s.

manifestoes
ideology
polemics

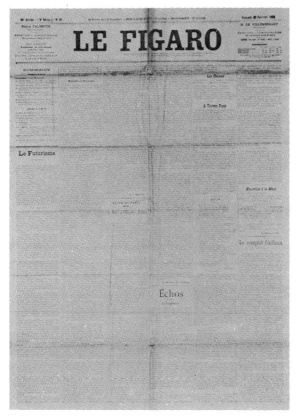

An extract from the Futurist Manifesto in 'Le Figaro', 20th February, 1909.

the dinner at the 'penna d'oca' and the manifesto of futurist cooking

From the very beginning of the Italian Futurist Movement 23 years ago (February 1909) the importance of food for the creative, reproductive, aggressive capacity of the human race excited the leading Futurists. It was often discussed by Marinetti, Boccioni, Sant'Elia, Russolo and Balla among themselves. In Italy and France there were a few attempts at a culinary renewal. Then on 15 November 1930 the need for a solution suddenly became urgent.

The PENNA D'OCA restaurant in Milan, run by Mario Tapparelli, offered the Milanese Futurists a banquet which would be a gastronomic eulogy of Futurism.

This *lista di vivande:*

oie grasse
ice cream on the moon
tears of the god 'Gavi'
consumato of roses and sunshine
Mediterranean favourite zig,zug,zag
roast lamb in lion sauce
little salad at daybreak
blood of Bacchus 'from the Ricasoli estate'
well-tempered little artichoke wheels
spun sugar rain
exhilarating 'cinzano' foam
fruit gathered in Eve's garden
coffee and liqueurs

very much pleased the guests: His Excellency Fornaciari, Prefect of Milan, Academician Marinetti, the Rt. Hon. Farinacci, the Rt.Hon. Sansanelli, Academician Giordano, Umberto Notari, Pick Mangiagalli, Chiarelli, Steffenini, Repaci, Ravasio, and the Futurists Depero, Prampolini, Escodamè, Gerbino, etc.

The least Futurist among them applauded the most. And this was logical, for except for the broth of roses which intoxicated the Futurist palates of

Marinetti, Prampolini, Depero, Escodamè and Gerbino, the dishes seemed only timidly original and still tied to gastronomic tradition. Bulgheroni, the chef, was repeatedly acclaimed.

Marinetti, invited to speak into a little radio microphone placed on the table between the 'well-tempered little artichoke wheels' and the 'spun sugar rain', said:

'I hereby announce the imminent launch of Futurist Cooking to renew totally the Italian way of eating and fit it as quickly as possible to producing the new heroic and dynamic strengths required of the race. Futurist cooking will be free of the old obsession with volume and weight and will have as one of its principles the abolition of pastasciutta. Pastasciutta, however agreeable to the palate, is a passéist food because it makes people heavy, brutish, deludes them into thinking it is nutritious, makes them sceptical, slow, pessimistic. Besides which patriotically it is preferable to substitute rice.'

This speech provoked wild applause, irritation and misgiving among the guests. Marinetti braved ironies in making his thought plain.

The next day a violent controversy broke out in all the newspapers, with participants from every social category, from society ladies to cooks, literary men, astronomers, doctors, street urchins, nursemaids, soldiers, peasants, dockers. Whenever pasta was served in any restaurant, inn or home in Italy it was immediately interlaced with interminable discussions.

●

On 28 December 1930 there appeared in the Gazzetta del Popolo in Turin

the Manifesto of futurist cooking

'Italian Futurism, father of numerous Futurisms and avant-gardeisms abroad, will not remain a prisoner of those worldwide victories secured 'in twenty years of great artistic and political battles frequently consecrated in blood,' as Benito Mussolini put it. Italian Futurism will face unpopularity again with a programme for the total renewal of food and cooking.

Of all artistic and literary movements Futurism is the only one whose essence is reckless audacity. Twentieth-century painting and twentieth-century literature are in reality two very moderate and practical Futurisms of the right. Attached to tradition, dependent on each other, they prudently only essay the new.

Cover of 'Les mots en liberté
futuristes', Edizioni futuriste di
poesia, Milan.

Marinetti's notepaper.

A selection of Futurist manifestoes.

Against pasta

Futurism has been defined by the philosophers as *'mysticism in action'*, by Benedetto Croce as *'anti-historicism'*, by Graça Aranha as *'liberation from aesthetic terror'*. We call it *'the renewal of Italian pride'*, a formula for *'original art-life'*, *'the religion of speed'*, *'mankind straining with all his might towards synthesis'*, *'spiritual hygiene'*, *'a method of infallible creation'*, *'the geometric splendour of speed'*, *'the aesthetics of the machine'*.

Against practicality we Futurists therefore disdain the example and admonition of tradition in order to invent at any cost something *new* which everyone considers crazy.

While recognizing that badly or crudely nourished men have achieved great things in the past, we affirm this truth: men think dream and act according to what they eat and drink.

Let us consult on this matter our lips, tongue, palate, taste buds, glandular secretions and probe with genius into gastric chemistry.

We Futurists feel that for the male the voluptuousness of love is an abysmal excavator hollowing him out from top to bottom, whereas for the female it works horizontally and fan-wise. The voluptuousness of the palate, however, is for both men and women always an upward movement through the human body. We also feel that we must stop the Italian male from becoming a solid leaden block of blind and opaque density. Instead he should harmonize more and more with the Italian female, a swift spiralling transparency of passion, tenderness, light, will, vitality, heroic constancy. Let us make our Italian bodies agile, ready for the featherweight aluminium trains which will replace the present heavy ones of wood iron steel.

Convinced that in the probable future conflagration those who are most agile, most ready for action, will win, we Futurists have injected agility into world literature with words-in-liberty and simultaneity. We have generated surprises with illogical syntheses and dramas of inanimate objects that have purged the theatre of boredom. Having enlarged sculptural possibility with anti-realism, having created geometric architectonic splendour without decorativism and made cinematography and photography abstract, we will now establish the way of eating best suited to an ever more high speed, airborne life.

Above all we believe necessary:

a) The abolition of pastasciutta, an absurd Italian gastronomic religion.

It may be that a diet of cod, roast beef and steamed pudding is beneficial to the English, cold cuts and cheese to the Dutch and sauerkraut, smoked [salt] pork and sausage to the Germans, but pasta is not beneficial to the Italians. For example it is completely hostile to the vivacious spirit and passionate, generous, intuitive soul of the Neapolitans. If these people have been heroic fighters, inspired artists, awe-inspiring orators, shrewd lawyers, tenacious farmers it was in spite of their voluminous daily plate of pasta. When they eat it they develop that typical ironic and sentimental scepticism which can often cut short their enthusiasm.

A highly intelligent Neapolitan Professor, Signorelli, writes: 'In contrast to bread and rice, pasta is a food which is swallowed, not masticated. Such starchy food should mainly be digested in the mouth by the saliva but in this case the task of transformation is carried out by the pancreas and the liver. This leads to an interrupted equilibrium in these organs. From such disturbances derive lassitude, pessimism, nostalgic inactivity and neutralism.'

An invitation to chemistry

Pastasciutta, 40 % less nutritious than meat, fish or pulses, ties today's Italians with its tangled threads to Penelope's slow looms and to somnolent old sailing-ships in search of wind. Why let its massive heaviness interfere with the immense network of short long waves which Italian genius has thrown across oceans and continents? Why let it block the path of those landscapes of colour form sound which circumnavigate the world thanks to radio and television? The defenders of pasta are shackled by its ball and chain like convicted lifers or carry its ruins in their stomachs like archaeologists. And remember too that the abolition of pasta will free Italy from expensive foreign grain and promote the Italian rice industry.

b) The abolition of volume and weight in the conception and evaluation of food.

c) The abolition of traditional mixtures in favour of experimentation with new, apparently absurd mixtures, following the advice of Jarro Maincave and other Futurist cooks.

d) The abolition of everyday mediocrity from the pleasures of the palate.

We invite chemistry immediately to take on the task of providing the body with its necessary calories through equivalent nutrients provided free by the State, in powder or pills, albumoid compounds, synthetic fats and vitamins. This way we will achieve a real lowering of the cost of living and of salaries, with a relative reduction in working hours. Today only one workman is needed for two thousand kilowatts. Soon machines will constitute an obedient proletariat of iron steel aluminium at the service of men who are almost totally relieved of manual work. With work reduced to two or three hours, the other hours can be perfected and ennobled though study, the arts, and the anticipation of perfect meals.

In all social classes meals will be less frequent but perfect in their daily provision of equivalent nutrients.

The perfect meal requires:

1. Originality and harmony in the table setting (crystal, china, décor) extending to the flavours and colours of the foods.

2. Absolute originality in the food.

'Sculpted meat'

Example: to prepare *Alaskan Salmon in the rays of the sun with Mars sauce*, take a good Alaskan salmon, slice it and put the slices under the grill with pepper, salt and high quality oil until golden. Then add halved-tomatoes previously cooked under the grill with parsley and garlic.

Just before serving place on top of the slices some anchovy fillets interlaced in a chequerboard pattern. On every slice a wheel of lemon with capers. The sauce will be composed of anchovies, hard-boiled egg yolks, basil, olive oil and a little glass of Italian Aurum liqueur, all passed through a sieve. (Formula by Bulgheroni, head chef at the Penna d'Oca).

Example: To prepare the *Woodcock Mount Rosa with Venus sauce*, take a good woodcock, clean it, cover its stomach with slices of prosciutto and fat bacon, put it in a casserole with butter, salt, pepper and juniper berries and cook in a very hot oven for 15 minutes, basting it with cognac. Remove from the pan and place immediately on a large square slice of bread soaked in rum and cognac, and cover it with puff pastry. Then put it back into the oven until the pastry is well cooked. Serve it with this sauce: half a glass of marsala and white wine, four tablespoons of bilberries and some finely-chopped orange peel, boiled together for 10 minutes. Put the sauce in the sauce boat and serve it very hot. (Formula by Bulgheroni, head chef at the Penna d'Oca).

3)The invention of appetizing food sculptures, whose original harmony of form and colour feeds the eyes and excites the imagination before it tempts the lips.

Example: the *Sculpted meat* created by the Futurist painter Fillìa, a symbolic interpretation of all the varied landscapes of Italy, is composed of a large cylindrical rissole of minced veal stuffed with eleven different kinds of cooked green vegetables and roasted. This cylinder, standing upright in the centre of the plate, is crowned by a layer of honey and supported at the base by a ring of sausages resting on three golden spheres of chicken.

Equator + North Pole

Example: The edible food sculpture *Equator + North Pole* created by the Futurist painter Enrico Prampolini is composed of an equatorial sea of poached egg yolks seasoned like oysters with pepper, salt and lemon. In the centre emerges a cone of firmly whipped egg white full of orange segments looking like juicy sections of the sun. The peak of the cone is strewn with pieces of black truffle cut in the form of black aeroplanes conquering the zenith.

These flavourful colourful perfumed and tactile food sculptures will form perfect simultaneous meals.

4) The abolition of the knife and fork for eating food sculptures, which can give prelabial tactile pleasure.

5) The use of the art of perfumes to enhance tasting.

Every dish must be preceded by a perfume which will be driven from the table with the help of electric fans.

6) The use of music limited to the intervals between courses so as not to distract the sensitivity of the tongue and palate but to help annul the last taste enjoyed by re-establishing gustatory virginity.

7) The abolition of speech-making and politics at the table.

8) The use in prescribed doses of poetry and music as surprise ingredients to accentuate the flavours of a given dish with their sensual intensity.

9) The rapid presentation, between courses, under the eyes and nostrils of the guests, of some dishes they will eat and others they will not, to increase their curiosity, surprise and imagination.

10) The creation of simultaneous and changing canapés which contain ten, twenty flavours to be tasted in a few seconds. In Futurist cooking these canapes have by analogy the same amplifying function that images have in literature. A given taste of something can sum up an entire area of life, the history of an amorous passion or an entire voyage to the Far East.

11) A battery of scientific instruments in the kitchen: *ozonizers* to give liquids and foods the perfume of ozone, *ultra-violet ray lamps* (since many foods when irradiated with ultra-violet rays acquire active properties, become more assimilable, preventing rickets in young children, etc.), *electrolyzers* to decompose juices and extracts, etc. in such a way as to obtain from a known product a new product with new properties, *colloidal mills* to pulverize flours, dried fruits, drugs, etc.; *atmospheric and vacuum stills, centrifugal autoclaves, dialyzers.* The use of these appliances will have to be scientific, avoiding the typical error of cooking foods under steam pressure, which provokes the destruction of active substances (vitamins etc.) because of the high temperatures. *Chemical indicators* will take into account the acidity and alkalinity of the sauces and serve to correct possible errors: too little salt, too much vinegar, too much pepper or too much sugar.

F.T. MARINETTI

●

As the debate for and against pasta and for and against Futurist foods raged worldwide, the paper 'La Cucina italiana', edited with great talent and ability by Umberto and Delia Notari, began an investigation.

Among the many defenders of pastasciutta were the learned doctors Bettazzi, Foa, Pini, Lombroso, Ducceschi, Londono and Viale, etc. Most un-scientifically they obeyed the dictates of their palates. They seemed to be speaking from a table in some trattoria in Posillipo, with their mouths blissfully full of *spaghetti alle vongole*. They do not have the spiritual lucidity of the laboratory. They forget the lofty dynamic obligations of the race and the searing speed and most violent contradictory forces that constitute the agonizing rush of modern life.

While making a great effort to legitimize what their mouths prefer, they have to admit that other foods are at least as nutritious as pasta.

Some of them say that perfumes and music etc. can only be compared to stimulants, whereas we consider them as actions to create in the diner an optimistic state of mind singularly conducive to a good digestion. And not only that: the perfumes, music and tactilisms which season Futurist foods bring about that playful and virile state of mind indispensable after lunch and at night.

All the defenders of pasta and implacable enemies of Futurist cooking are melancholy types, content with their melancholy and propagandists of melancholy.

Any pastasciuttist who honestly examines his conscience at the moment he ingurgitates his biquotidian pyramid of pasta will find within the gloomy satis-faction of stopping up a black hole. This voracious hole is an incurable sad-ness of his. He may delude himself, but nothing can fill it. Only a Futurist meal can lift his spirits.

And pasta is anti-virile because a heavy, bloated stomach does not encourage physical enthusiasm for a woman, nor favour the possibility of possessing her at any time.

But in the same investigation medical men spoke up who radiated intelligence:
   'the habitual and exaggerated use of pasta certainly causes obesity and exaggerated abdominal volume.'
   'the great consumers of pasta have slow and pacific characters, while meat eaters are quick and aggressive.'
                                        Prof. NICOLA PENDE (clinician).

'to vary our foods is a biological law; experience shows that constant repetition of the same food is a cause of damage.'

Prof. Senator U. GABBI (clinician).

'I believe that the use of pasta may be harmful to intellectual workers, to people who lead a sedentary life and, above all, to people who allow themselves meat and other dishes as well.'

Prof. Senator ALBERTONI.

'It's a matter of taste and of the price in the market. In any case the best thing is a mixed diet and never one based on a single food.'

Prof. A. HERLITZKA (physiologist).

'the nutritive value of pastasciutta does not offer any special characteristics that might make it preferable to those of other types of farinaceous foods.'

Prof. ANTONIO RIVA (clinician).

'Pasta cannot be considered a food which is easily digested because it dilates the stomach and unlike bread does not undergo a sufficient preparation through mastication.'

Prof. Dr. C. TARCHETTI.

●

Further investigations, for and against pasta, were conducted by the 'Giornale della Domenica' in Rome and other Italian newspapers. The Duke of Bovino, Mayor of Naples, in response to one of these inquiries, declared that 'the Angels in Paradise eat nothing but vermicelli with tomato sauce', consecrating the unappetising monotony of Paradise and of the life of the Angels.

In the meantime, the controversy spread with hundreds of articles. Take, for example, those written by Massimo Bontempelli, Paolo Monelli, Paolo Buzzi, Arturo Rossato, Angelo Frattini, Salvatore di Giacomo, etc.

Take the various opinions of the Roman chefs Giaquinto, Paggi, Alfredo, Cecchino, 'Sister Elvira', etc., all of them, being unable to revolutionize their cooking, sided with pastasciutta.

Take the issue of 'Travaso' in Rome wholly dedicated to Futurist cooking and the innumerable cartoons that appeared in 'Guerin Meschino,' 'Marc' Aurelio', '420', 'Giovedì' etc., etc.

But while the enemies of Futurist cooking contented themselves with facile ironies and nostalgic whining, support and enthusiasm for the struggle against pasta grew apace.

Of all the articles, the one by Ramperti, published in 'Ambrosiano' as 'An Open Letter to F.T. Marinetti', wins hands down:

My Dear Friend,

Do you remember you once wrote that I, Marco Ramperti, belonged to the extreme right of the Futurist parliament? You are amiability in person, my dear Marinetti, notwithstanding all the fights and scuffles in your dialectic of attack, and you could not have spoken more graciously of one who, though he listens to you and is your friend, has his own ideas, which are not always those of tactilism and words-in-liberty. You wanted to be kind to me, and you gave me a little place on your right, among those who might be converted, when you might very well have left me outside the door among the irremediable, unentitled passéists. Since that day, I must confess, several times your law-decrees have put me in the cruel dilemma of either handing you my resignation or demanding yours, so great were the differences in our opinions, making my presence insupportable in your assembly. Then along came your convivial rebellion, your manifesto against pasta: and lo and behold, reanimated, illuminated, re-made in a moment full of audacity in good faith, your pallid Futurist *ad honorem* moved in one bound from the extreme right to the extreme left of your assizes, and bless me if he didn't cry out to you his full, absolute, fanatical, desperate agreement.

Although, alas, I am not the youngest of your regiment, I ask you now, Marinetti, if I may carry the banner of this latest offensive of yours. It seems to me that the food revolution is the most providential of all you have ever embarked upon. In fact it seems the most difficult. You see how the Italians, touched in the epigastrium, already rebel against you. They may accept tactilism, words-in-liberty, noise intoners. But they won't give up pasta. They accept fighting, leaping and running: but only with their serving of spaghetti. They accept, and understand, the need to regain primacy in the world: nevertheless they are prepared to cede this priority for a heap of macaroni, as Esau did for a mess of pottage. You see how these people of ours are made, unfortunately. They are capable of giving up all comforts, all advantages, but not their appetite. Ah, Marinetti, you shouldn't believe that this time the battle will be easy! That's precisely why I beg the honour of serving you. Believe me: we will need courage. People will jeer; pasta will return to the table; and we will have to preach for who knows how long to full bellies and empty hearts.

No matter. Victory will be all the better for coming late, as in all good revolutions. Our revolution will meanwhile spread its word, establish its jurisdiction. Since the Italians have agreed to the Futurist principle of making themselves as far as possible nimble, wide-awake, quick, electric, furious, we shall see the day when they are convinced that to reach such a state of grace nothing serves better than to eat little and with discrimination, and to limit meals to the essential drop of liquid and the leonine crumb. Really, Marinetti, your latest propaganda campaign is the most important and logical of all those which stemmed from your cardinal manifesto of 20 years ago: and so much resistance to it would be incomprehensible if one did not remember the mulish obstinacy of certain habits of the stomach. It's not the first time a nation has learnt to give up everything except gluttony. The Count of Gobineau, a Frenchman who thought highly of the Germans, used to say that the other side of the Rhine nobody knew how to commit a crime except for sausage and sauerkraut. It's a judgement that reminds me of that Pulcinella who could resist everything except a handful of vermicelli. This grand passion for pasta is an Italian weakness, and you have a hundred reasons for crushing it to pieces. Here is the Achilles heel, and there is the Futurist palate. Now, among all the bloating and stultifying foods that are at variance with your programme of speed, elasticity and energy, pasta is precisely the most widespread and disastrous. But although it does the most harm, it is the least damned. And that's the mainspring of your reparative revolt. What does it mean, this or that habit, this or that vice, this or that vileness? We should also liberate ourselves from pasta, which is also a form of slavery. It puffs out our cheeks like grotesque masks on a fountain, it stuffs our gullets as if we were Christmas turkeys, it ties up our insides with its flabby strings; it nails us to the chair, gorged and stupefied, apoplectic and gasping, with that sensation of uselessness which, depending on the individual, brings pleasure or shame, but in any case must be abhorred by anyone boasting a Futurist spirit or anyone young and alert.

In short, my dear Marinetti, you have understood perfectly the danger and disgrace of this myth of maccheroni: this *macaroni* as they call it abroad which has made us the butt of indecorous metaphors beyond the Alps. Once it was said we ate spaghetti with our hands: and perhaps the sense of that slander was that such gluttony could not be separated from slovenliness and dirty habits. Then they conceded us forks, perhaps in order to have the right to say at Geneva that even the Italians go armed to the teeth; but spaghetti was not removed from our folkloristic picture. Today all Europe knows how many helpings Primo Carnera eats, just as they knew in 1894 how much Francesco Crispi devoured. The allegorical Italian has always got his avid mouth wide open over a plate of tagliatelle when he isn't dangling dripping strands of vermicelli down his greedy gullet. And it's an offensive image: derisory, grotesque, ugly. It's designed to show up the vanity of that appetite of ours, together with its bestial impetuosity. Basically, pasta does not nourish. It is filling: but it doesn't freshen the blood. Its substance is minimal compared to its volume. But that, our allegorical detractors would say, is just what makes it a real Italian dish. Our pasta is like our rhetoric, only good for filling up our mouths. Its enjoyment lies entirely in the way it forces the jaws wide open, the way it demands voluptuous self-abandonment, the way it sticks to the palate and the intestines, the way the eater feels he has become one with it, knotted into a sticky ball and re-fashioned. But it's a piggish enjoyment. It's a short-lived bliss. Swallowed down the way it is, spaghetti poisons us and weighs us down. We suddenly feel as leaden as false coins. Something jams us up, down below, like a log. We have no more easy syllables or ready images. Our thoughts wind round each other, get mixed up and tangled like the vermicelli we've taken in. Words get knotted into a sticky ball in the same way. The only piquancy on our lips is tomato.

Heaven help us if we are about to enter a discussion or join a lover. Rhymes are fatuous, witticisms cretinous, reasoning impossible, when tremors of the bowel disturb them. We know that the sins of the gullet are those most quickly punished by the Old Man in the Sky. The sin of pasta is expiated instantly. The stomach expands at the expense of the brain. All spirit, witty or amorous, is enchained or exiled. After a feast of tagliatelle just try going to a discussion. Or to Cythera. I bet you stop after the first few metres, if you haven't already been exhausted by getting to your feet. How much paradise lost, for a moment of mindless animality!

....

●

MARCO RAMPERETI

V.G. PENNINO,

leading columnist on the 'Gazzetta del Popolo' enters the debate with the following letter to F.T. Marinetti:

'As a fervent admirer of yours since I was a boy, when I followed with passionate interest the purifying battles you fought against the indifference and incomprehension of the Italians of the day, I read with enthusiasm your manifesto of Futurist Cooking. It's certainly true we think dream and act according to what we eat and drink, just as it's certainly true − with regard to nourishment − that even today people are still arguing with one another amid uncertainties, contradictions and errors of every kind. It seems that the main preoccupation of those who cook is to stuff, to fill the stomach as one fills a sack, to excite it and poison it with drugs and evil concoctions, *while it ought to be to prepare healthy, energizing, delicious food, pleasant to the eye to the touch to the palate, food which in small quantities strengthens and nourishes,* food which awakens the imagination with rural panoramas, scents of tropical gardens and which induces dreams without resort to alcoholic beverages. Blessed be, therefore, the renewing and revitalizing gust of wind in the heavy atmosphere of the kitchens of Italy, blessed be the struggle against this deadly pasta which weighs down the body and numbs the spirit with its exhausting digestions. (Note that I am a Neapolitan and have known all the evils of this food.) When encumbering and soporific pasta is banned from the tables of the peninsula, when the kitchen is no longer the dominion of inept housewives and ignorant, poisoning cooks, but becomes a source of wise chemical combinations and aesthetic sensations, *when we succeed in creating and diffusing a way of eating that can reconcile tiny quantities with maximum explosive dynamic nutritive power*, only then will the will-power, vitality, imagination and creative genius of the race reach its apogee.

But the struggle against pasta is not enough. We need to pull down other idols, uproot erroneous traditions: *to affirm that white bread*, for example, heavy and tasteless, *is a useless food* which forms an indigestible mass in the stomach and should be replaced by wholegrain bread, fragrant and substantial; *that rice is a precious food*, but only as long as it is not deprived of its organic qualities by polishing; *that vegetables contain real treasures* for the human organism (iron, phosphorus, vitamins, globulin, calcium, potassium and magnesium salts, etc.) as long as these treasures are not stupidly destroyed through absurd cooking and that, in short, the theory of calories and of the need for large amounts of animal proteins and fats has had its day and that it's now recognized that a small quantity of food, well combined according to the intelligent recognition of the needs of our organism gives much more strength and energy than the macaroni, meat and egg dishes consumed by those who wish *to sustain themselves*. Every nation must have its own way of eating and *that of the Italian people must be based on the produce of this warm, restless, volcanic land*; it should therefore be three-quarters composed of the marvellous vegetable products for which we are envied throughout the world and a scant quarter of animal products. These must be used very frugally, especially by intellectual workers, while soldiers, manual workers and in general those who engage in a great deal of physical activity can eat more of it (the opposite of what normally happens). It is well that people should know a raw carrot finely chopped with oil and lemon, a plate of onions or olives or a combination of these things, together with a few nuts and slice of brown bread, are a much more suitable and useful fuel for the human stove than the notorious *maccheroni al ragù* or *tagliatelli alla bolognese* or *beefsteaks à la Bismarck*. Moreover with the simpler, healthier wholefoods one can create dishes that give the eyes, the palate and the imagination much more intense sensations than the foods which today make a pretty show on the best tables.

'So the battle you have engaged in – even though it seems very hard, because it must clash with deeply-rooted and obstinate traditions, with formidable interests and widespread ignorance – must find a great deal of agreement in the Italy of today, for in seeking to renew a stagnant world environment too strongly rooted in the past *it has enormous social and economical importance*, especially if the invitation you issued to the world of chemistry is welcomed by Italian scientists. A French chemist – Prof. Mono – has invented some 'concentrated foods' whose efficacy I have tested, but they have the problem of being, above all, foreign and also fairly expensive. Let's hope that some Italian chemists will find out how to make more of these and better.

'Excuse me for having allowed myself to send you these hasty notes, suggested to me by your very beautiful manifesto, but I thought, among the very many responses you will undoubtedly receive, that you would not be displeased to know of the enthusiastic agreement of a modest scholar of the problems of nutrition.'

G.V. PENNINO

●

Of the many articles that appeared in support of the Futurist struggle against pasta we note the most original:

the head chef to the king

The Cavaliere Pettini, head chef to His Majesty the King of Italy, speaks precisely on the subject: 'It is beyond doubt that all farinaceous foods weigh the body down and in consequence... are a threat to the intelligence' and also, in his letter to the paper 'La Cucina italiana' he again affirms 'the necessity of innovations, of modernism in cooking too, a business which must also respond to the times and even lead them.'

Schopenhauer and pasta

Dr. Angelo Vasta, in an article on Futurist food, observes: 'The Neapolitans have rebelled, but that is why it is a good idea to recall what their fellow citizen Dr. Carito wrote in 'Umanità Artritica': ...the mass of our people are still in a primitive stage. All in all, they haven't made great progress since the time when Schopenhauer, observing their daily diet, brilliantly styled it *the food of the resigned*.

'Alas, even our upper classes, the intellectuals, even the so-called 'leaders' don't know how to feed themselves properly. Hence the torpor of their physiological life with its inevitable harmful reverberations in the psychical sphere. Hence that notorious 'indolence' for which we have been singled out and reviled over the last centuries. In everything concerning our nutrition, exercise and sporting activity we have to reform ourselves radically...'

a sixteenth-century medical man against pasta

In an article in 'Secolo XIX', of Genoa, Amedeo Pescio rebels against those who call ravioli, lasagne, taglierini etc. the glory and pride of the Genoese. And he writes: 'Giovanni da Vigo began the campaign against pasta in the 1500s, when as a good and very gifted man from Rapallo he cured popes and princes, prelates and ministers, dynamic people, who would *no sooner* have tried to digest a basketful of trenette than they would a bag of coal. This great surgeon of *our city* (as he said, speaking of Genoa) wrote 'The Practice of the Art of Surgery'. In the IXth and last book there is an explicit, formal warning against the abuse of pasta; the recommendation, the almost Marinettian prescription for a bloated sixteenth century: *all the pasta dishes must be used very infrequently* 'pasti alia denique et victualia paste rarissime sunt concedenda'.

pasta originated
with the ostrogoths

Libero Glauco Silvano, in a long article 'A Contribution to a Futurist Culinary Art' proposed some innovations in eating. We reproduce here the part of his amusing article against pasta:

'For Heaven's sake, wasn't it time to do something about that barbaric food which had only survived by scrounging off our ultramodern civilization: I'm speaking of macaroni in a sauce, with tomatoes or however you like it. This dish, surely more bestial than any other, looks to us like a female chimpanzee in a sentimental ladies' drawing room: and it's only through a mistaken respect for tradition that people have continued to tolerate its plebeian stench. The name itself recalls the rough, greasy, filthy people in whose midst it was born: macaroni.' A few well-meaning chefs, disciples and emulators of Brillat-Savarin, finally managed to gentrify him, by shaking off his tango of scumbag companions: they pledged him not to seek the company of certain puffed-up and uncouth onions, fat as sailor's sweethearts, and certain bulbs of garlic, bleached and shrivelled by hidden diseases, and rancid and goatish oil. But under his new clothes there still lurked the manners and vulgarities of a spruced-up peasant and his continued frequenting of that gracious epicurean gentleman called butter meant nothing to him. He still had the same rumbling and intrusive belly; and wherever he appeared, in the houses of the rich or the poor, he looked around him, wanting to impose respect and reverence, as if he were descended from far too noble a family not to rate the other gastronomic creatures below nothing.

But what were his noble entitlements to grace, pray? Fortunately we have Dacovio Saraceno's 'Chronicle of Memorabilia' which recounts his life and miracles: 'Macaroni was born and raised among the Ostrogoths who often enjoyed comforting themselves with him. The said macaroni was a kind of wheat (read: spelt) and his first home was in the kingdom of the great prince Theodore, that is in Ravenna, who entrusted him to the care of Rotufo, his brilliant cook. The subjects of the kingdom grew to know him thanks to the cook's wife who had taken a fancy to the Officer of the Guard at the palace and to whom, between a little kiss here and a peck there she revealed the existence of the said macaroni. Thus love for this macaroni spread among the whole population; and they boiled him with onions and garlic and parsnips and they seasoned him with gherkin jus (sic); and they licked their fingers and their snouts.'

Ah, what gentle little ladies they were, who licked their fingers and snouts! That monstrous food seasoned with gherkin juice was well-suited to their hardened palates. I can just see them, those moustachioed Ostrogoths, setting themselves to gouge out great holes in the grass with their heavy daggers and then squatting round them, wiping their mouths on the ends of their moustaches in seraphic anticipation. Then their worthy consorts, worn and filthy, come and empty into these improvized bowls a slimy heap of worms called 'macaroni' and their hairy arms plunge into the fuming hole up to the elbow and their mouths open wide — gobble gobble — and tears run down their grimy cheeks in an excess of bliss.

It was only in the high Middle Ages (Cordazio Camaldolese: *The Main Dishes in Use in our Lands and Regions and Islands and Peninsulas and so on With their Manner of Preparation in the Kitchen Explained*) that gherkins were replaced by tomatoes, the cultivation of which was already quite extensive, dating from when Brother Serenio, on his return from China, brought that most precious seed — and not the seed of the silkworm, as is commonly believed (cf. in this regard the definitive work of historical exegesis written by Valbo Scaravacio and entitled 'Truth and Nonsense', published by Pirocchi, publishers in the Old Town: Sant'Anselobio, price 8 carlins.) An immensely detailed and long-winded biography of Boccaccio informs us that the author of the Decameron had his wife dress the macaroni with bitter almond milk: 'But', says the biographer, 'the esteemed author still could not digest it.' I suggest that this was perhaps because Boccaccio had too much good taste to accept this dish calmly; and that whatever way he had it prepared, his aristocratic palate would have refused it. Nevertheless, willingly or not, he swallowed the macaroni down because the tradition was so deeply-rooted not even he could imagine doing without it.

In the last part of the Renaissance the damned dish just missed being buried in oblivion. It was scarcely ever mentioned any more, but then up popped that mischievous gossip Aretino who put it back on the altar. And what method of propaganda could be better than his very provocative flesh and blood muses?

Many of those who dined at his table became fervent partisans of macaroni and one of them, to make himself worthy in the eyes of his honoured Lord, actually composed a collection of sonnets singing the praises of the food 'beside which ambrosia itself is nothing'; he was by chance Marione Dagorazzi and his hundred poetical verses were entitled 'Earthly Ambrosia'.

Towards the end of the eighteenth century many noble minds, convinced that the cause of a great number of ills was to be sought in that dish, began a vigorous campaign to shake the yoke of slavery from humanity's shoulders. Innumerable pamphlets and tomes of various sizes were written: the most widely-read newspapers contained articles by people who had acquired great authority in the field of science and letters: but nothing could prevail against the indifference of the common people, also because at that time the superstition was widespread that macaroni was the antidote for every disease, the universal panacea. A last attempt was made in the first half of the nineteenth century by the great Michael Scrofetta, whose merits are too well-known to speak of here; yet even this eminent scientist could achieve nothing concrete.

It has fallen to our epoch definitively to repudiate this barbarous eating habit. We, children of the century and so free from prejudice, can send macaroni and its accessories packing without so much as a help yourself: and no one will grieve or shed tender tears, even those who have as it were unthinkingly eaten macaroni three times a day, morning, noon and night. Ugh! What piggish stuff, macaroni: to get the message across paintings, prints, photographs and everything that happens to depict it must vanish from our houses: and publishers must recall all their books from the shops to subject them to rigorous censorship, deleting without pity, reprinting on the spot where necessary. In a few months just hearing it named – macaroni, ugh! – people will throw up.

However, I would like to think that this victory, remarkable as it may be, will not let us rest on our laurels. There are other dishes which, on close examination, show themselves unworthy of praise from gourmets or solid heads of families and their thoughtful offspring. Indeed it is my conviction that enormous cuts must be made in old recipe books. Our housewives go on preparing foods in the old way because they don't know otherwise. They sense dimly that this or that method isn't right but they don't know to what other saint to pledge themselves. But now the first nucleus of scholars has emerged to try to create a cuisine adapted to our times. The task is colossal: to destroy something only one hand is needed to light the fuse, but to rebuild it thousands and thousands of hands are necessary.

The battle
for the sanity, agility and freshness
of Italian intellectualism

Ferdinando Collai, Head of the Press Office in Bologna attacks 'the flabby pacifying congesting argumentations of the most illustrious representatives of the starchy world, the rot-gut block of ruinously overpraised Neopolitan or Bolognese pasta'. And he concludes: 'I am with the Master in the violent struggle for the health, agility and freshness of Italian intellectualism.'

Pastasciutta
is not the food for fighters

Paolo Monelli, in defence of pasta, declares it the ideal food for the fighting man. Perhaps this was true for the Alpinists who, of all soldiers, after battles, escapades and avalanches are the most ready to improvise perfect equipment, comfortable huts, well-stocked and furnished barracks and expert kitchens. But this is not true for the troops who fight on the plain. The Futurists who fought at Doberdò, at Selo, on the Vertoibizza, at Plava and at the Case di Zagora and afterwards at Casa Dus, Nervese and Capo Sile are ready to testify that they always ate the most awful pasta, delayed and transformed into a cold, congealed mass by the artillery barrages of the enemy which separated the orderlies and cooks from the warriors. Who could have hoped for hot pasta *al dente*? Marinetti, wounded at the Case di Zagora in the May 1917 offensive and transported down to Plava on a stretcher, received a miraculous chicken broth from a soldier who was an ex-cook of Savini's: that sagacious cook, however, though he came along at just the right time and was zealous and devoted to a former client he liked, could not, with the best will in the world, have offered him an edible pasta, since terrible Austrian shells were crashing down on the batallion kitchen every now and again and smashing his stoves. Marinetti had his first doubts then on the suitability of pasta as a food for war. For the bombardiers of the Vertoibizza like Marinetti the usual food was a lump of chocolate smeared with mud and sometimes a horsemeat steak, cooked in a frying pan that had been washed out with eau de Cologne.

●

Apart from these many declarations of support from cooks, hygienists and artists, the controversy about Futurist cooking gave birth to a whole series of articles and studies on the quality of 'rice', an Italian food which must continue to be further popularized and utilized.

World opinion

The debate on Futurist Cooking burst upon Paris after Marinetti's Manifesto was published in the daily paper 'Comoedia' on 20th January 1931:

F.T. Marinetti
vient de lancer le manifeste de la cuisine futuriste' ...

●

And we give here a translation of the shrewd article written for *Comoedia* by the French journalist Audisio in support of Futurist cooking:

'Yes, pasta really is a dictatorship of the stomach, yes, it brings with it a torpor that borders on bliss, and it is indeed the succulent poison that ruins the liver for the greater joy of the stomach. We are not among those who despise it, we even love it ... but we distrust it especially if prepared the Roman way, which is to say, undercooked. Because to digest it is an insidious, slow process of rumination, inviting feeble imaginings, empty dreams, sceptical renunciation, in the unctuous conciliatory rhythm of the sloth.

Wash it down with Salerno or Frascati and you will understand the torpor of the cosy masses and of the prelates of Rome or Naples, which is also the origin of the languid sentimentalism, serene irony, amiable indifference, and transcendental wisdom with which eternal Rome, from Horace to Panzini, has defied the passing of time.

'Today we need to remake the Italian man, for what point is there in having him raise his arm in the Roman salute if he can rest it without effort on his bulging stomach? Modern man must have a flat stomach, under the sun, to think clearly, and he must be decisive and energetic: look at the Negro man, look at the Arab. Marinetti's gastronomic paradox aims at moral education just as his paradoxes in aesthetic education do: the matter must be shaken up to quicken the spirit.

A year ago we were saying that Marinetti castigated hypocritical modesty and intellectual dishonesty and now here he is scourging the hypocritical beatitude of the stomach. It is a whole moral philosophy that Marinetti is demolishing behind this culinary smokescreen. No doubt he is remembering the beautiful violent times when under a Parisian sky he planted the germ of a world revolution of the spirit.'

After the publications in the *Comoedia*, articles, comments, caricatures and discussions followed in the major French, English, American and German newspapers.

The interview with Marinetti in the paper *Je suis partout* and the in-depth article on the front page of the daily *Le Petit Marseillais* on Futurist cooking were the most important. The London *Times* returned to the controversy again and again with various articles, also publishing polemical poetry. There was a long article, 'ITALY MAY DOWN SPAGHETTI' in the *Chicago Tribune*. Other articles appeared in the Essen *Reinisch-Westfalische Zeitung* and the *Nieuwe Rotterdamsche Courant*. Newspapers from Budapest to Tunisia, from Tokyo to Sydney, revealed the importance of the Futurist battle 'against sadly wretched foods'.

This article which appeared in *The Herald* was among the first of them to stir up the debate on Futurist cooking.

Spaghetti for Italians, Knives and Forks for All are banned in Futurist Manifesto on Cooking

Marinetti, father of Futurist art, literature and drama, has just issued from Rome a manifesto launching Futurist cooking, according to word received yesterday in Paris. Practically everything connected with the traditional ppleasures of the gourmet will be swept away.

No more spaghetti for the Italians.

No more knives and forks.

No more after-dinner speeches will be tolerated by the new cult.

Details of the manifesto, published in the 'Comoedia', announce as the principal feature of the new cuisine a rapid sequence of dishes no bigger than a mouthful or even less than a mouthful.

In fact, in the ideal Futuristic meal, a certain number of dishes will be passed beneath the nose of the diner in order to excite his curiosity or provide a suitable contrast, and such supplementary courses will not be eaten at all.

'Since everything in modern civilization tends towards elimination of weight, and increased speed, the cooking of the future must conform to the ends of evolution. The first step will be the elimination of edible pastes from the diet of Italians', Marinetti writes.

Modern science will be employed in the preparation of sauces and a device similar to litmus paper will be used in a Futuristic kitchen in order to determine the proper degree of acidity or alkalinity in any given sauce.

Music will be banished from the table except in rare instances when it will be used to sustain the mood of a former course until the next can be served.

The new Futuristic meal will permit a literary influence to pervade the dining-room, for with ideal rapid service, by means of single successive mouthfuls, an experience such as a love affair or a journey can be suggested.

Among the new kitchen and dining-room instruments suggested by Marinetti is an 'ozonizer' which will give to liquids the taste and perfume of ozone, also ultra-violet lamps to render certain chemicals in the cooking more active.

Also certain dishes will be cooked under high pressure, in order to vary the effects of heat. Electrolysis will also be used to decompose sugar and other extracts.

As a model for the presentation of a Futuristic meal, M. Marinetti calls attention to a Futuristic painting by Fillìa, of a synthetic landscape made up of food-stuffs. The landscape is composed of roast veal, stuffed with eleven kinds of vegetables, placed vertically upon a plate and crowned with honey.

This is one of the meals which, under the new system, could not be attacked with a knife and fork and cut into haphazard sections before being eaten.

Besides the abolition of macaroni, Marinetti advocates doing away with the ordinary condiments now in use, and a consistent lightening of weight and reduction of volume of food-stuffs. The Futurist leader also pleads for discontinuance of daily eating for pleasure.

For ordinary daily nourishment he recommends scientific nourishment by means of pills and powders, so that when a real banquet is spread it may be appreciated aesthetically.

Against the cuisine of Grand Hotels and Xenomania

Amongst the various cuisines prevalent today the one we consider the most detestable and repugnant is the international cuisine of grand hotels, which opens all large official banquets with a clear soup, on which float four or five limp balls of dough, and which ends with a gelatinous and trembling sweet most suited to the mouths of invalids.

It is logical that politicians of every country who gather to discuss their great obligations, the revision of treaties, disarmament and the universal crisis, can clarify nothing and decide little after ingurgitating such depressing, saddening and monotonizing foods.

In Italy, as in almost every country in the world, we submit to this type of international grand hotel cuisine only because it comes from abroad. A bestial mania unfortunately dominates us, which we call *xenomania*, which we must fight against relentlessly. The *Gazzetta del Popolo* of 24th September 1931 published this Futurist manifesto by Marinetti against *xenomania*:

Against xenomania

A futurist manifesto addressed to the leaders of society and the intelligentsia

'Despite the Imperial strength of Fascism, the words *xenomania, xenomane*, which we have invented, are unfortunately becoming more indispensable every day.

1) Xenomanes and therefore guilty of anti-Italianism, are those young Italians

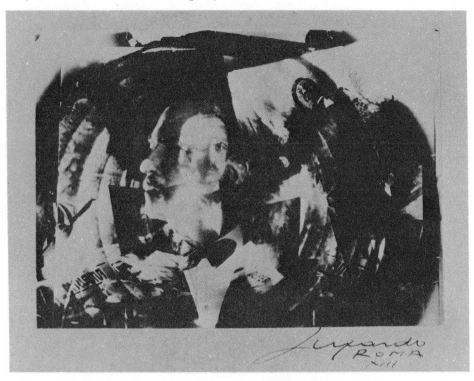

'*Ritratto di Marinetti*' by Elio Luxardo, 1935.

who fall into a cretinous ecstasy before all foreigners, even now the world crisis is robbing these people of their wealth; they fall in love with them out of snobbishness and sometimes marry them, absolving them from all defects (arrogance, bad manners, anti-Italianism, or ugliness) simply because they don't speak the Italian language and come from distant countries about which little or nothing is known.

2) Xenomanes and therefore guilty of anti-Italianism are world-famous Italian artistic performers (singers, musicians, orchestral conductors) when they grow so self-important that they forget the performer is the useful but not the necessary servant of creative genius. For example: the excellent and celebrated orchestral conductor Arturo Toscanini, who put his personal success before the prestige of his country by disowning his own national hymns in the name of artistic delicacy and opportunistically playing foreign anthems.

3) Xenomanes and therefore guilty of anti-Italianism are the Italian orchestral conductors and audiences who organize or applaud concerts abroad using little or no Italian music. Elementary patriotism demands that at least half the music on the programme should be by modern or Futurist Italian composers instead of music by Beethoven, Bach, Brahms, etc...., which is already enjoyed, understood and admired by everyone to the point of satiety.

4) Xenomanes and therefore guilty of anti-Italianism are the Italian audiences who applaud instead of booing foreign orchestra conductors when they are so ill-mannered as to ignore Italian music in their concerts in Italy.

5) Xenomanes and therefore guilty of anti-Italianism are the Italian industrialists who find a thousand reasons to avoid a decisive battle with foreign industry and are proud to win international competitions with products, machines or appliances not entirely conceived and made in Italy.

6) Xenomanes and therefore guilty of anti-Italianism are the military historians and critics who in our great victorious war dwell on negligible episodes such as Caporetto.

7) Xenomanes and therefore guilty of anti-Italianism are the illustrious men of letters who denigrate abroad the whole of Italian literature (which today is original, varied and entertaining), each one in the hope of appearing to be a very great genius amid a nation of mediocre illiterates.

8) Xenomanes and therefore guilty of anti-Italianism are the Italian painters, sculptors and architects who, like many twentieth-century personalities and

many rationalists, prefer to declare themselves heirs of French, Spanish and Swiss innovators like Cezanne, Picasso, Le Corbusier, rather than sons of real, authentic Italian innovators like Boccioni, creator of the new sculpture, and Sant'Elia, creator of the new architecture.

9) Xenomanes and therefore guilty of anti-Italianism are those public meetings which instead of branding as infamy the offensive writings and publications by Italian writers against Italy, our armed forces and our great victorious war, define them as 'permissible errors'.

10) Xenomanes and therefore guilty of anti-Italianism are the hoteliers and shopkeepers who ignore the prompt and effective means at their disposal to promote Italian influence in the world (by the use of Italian language in notices, on signs and on menus), forgetting that foreigners, in love with the country-side and climate of Italy, can also admire and study its language.

11) Xenomanes and therefore guilty of anti-Italianism are those aristocratic and upper middle-class Italian ladies who are infatuated with foreign customs and snobbisms. For example: the American snobbism surrounding alcohol and the fashion for *cocktail parties*, – perhaps suitable for the North American race but certainly poisonous to our race. Therefore we consider vulgar and foolish the Italian woman who proudly participates in *cocktail parties* and that sort of alcoholic competitiveness. Vulgar and foolish the Italian woman who thinks it more elegant to say 'I've drunk four cocktails' than 'I've eaten a bowl of minestrone'. She is only submitting herself to the foreigner's envied financial superiority, a superiority now destroyed by the world crisis.

Elegant Italian ladies, we beg that instead of the cocktail party you hold early-evening get-togethers which you could call, if you like, Mrs. B's Asti spumante, Countess C's Barbaresco or Princess D's White Capri. At these gatherings a prize will be given to the best wine for such meetings. And let's drop the word 'bar' and give it an Italian name: *quisibeve*.

12) Xenomanes and therefore guilty of anti-Italianism are the Italian men and women who give the Roman salute and then ask sentimentally for foreign products in the shops, casting a sceptical and pessimistic glance at Italian produce.

13) Xenomanes and therefore guilty of anti-Italianism are the Italian audiences who, seized by a critical mania, systematically disparage Italian films and theatre, thus encouraging the invasion of mediocre foreign films and plays.

14) Xenomanes and therefore guilty of anti-Italianism are the Italian impresarios who look abroad for stage designers and scene painters, neglecting the Italian ones, who are capable of teaching the world.

15) Xenomanes and therefore guilty of anti-Italianism are Italy's critics and cultivated gentlemen, whose brains were awakened and sharpened by Italian Futurism but who nonetheless criticize and neglect it in their rush to discover and praise foreign Futurisms, all derived from our own. As anti-Italians they forget, for example, this explicit statement made to an Italian journalist by the English Futurist poet Ezra Pound: 'The movement that I, Eliot, Joyce and others began in London could not have existed without Italian Futurism,' and this equally explicit declaration by Antoine in the Paris *Journal*: 'In the decorative arts the roads were opened some time ago by the school of Marinetti.'

Other nations, under-populated, and who are not criticized or menaced by foreign enemies, can doze in the drowsy hum of easily assuaged revolutionary plots and consider national pride an object of luxury.

But our virile proud dynamic and dramatic peninsula, envied and threatened on all sides, poised to realize its immense destiny, must consider national pride as its first law of life.

Therefore we Futurists, who twenty years ago cried at the top of our socially-democratically-communistically-clerically parliamentarily softened voices: 'The word Italy must rule over the word Liberty!', today proclaim:

a) The word Italy must rule over the word genius.
b) The word Italy must rule over the word intelligence.
c) The word Italy must rule over the words culture and statistics.
d) The word Italy must rule over the word truth.

The fire of criticism may be directed against foreign nations if necessary, but never against Italy.

Plenary indulgence in art and in life towards real patriots, that is to the Fascists who tremble with an authentic passion for Italy and with indefatigable Italian pride.

As for the many sceptics and defeatists (literary men, artists, philosophers and blue-stockings) who try today, amid the uncertainty of an unstable peace, to build one of their doubly careless ivory towers dedicated to the enemy, we say quite brutally:

Remember that Italy does not need to vaunt its distant past. Its grandeur lies in the present, based above all on the creative power of its poets and artists. Galileo, Volta, Ferraris, Marconi and the first transatlantic flight by a Fascist squadron, thought up by Mussolini and directed by Balbo, assure it supremacy in machine civilization. This supremacy certainly cannot belong to populous nations who banked on 'trust standard and over-production' who did not see the world crisis coming, and are now dying of it.

Always remember this Italian masterpiece which is even greater than the Divine Comedy: the battle 'Vittorio Veneto'.

In the name of this masterpiece, symbolized by the wreckage of the Austro-Hungarian Empire which our armoured divisions had to overpower on the road to Tarvisio, we, at the first alert, will shoot anti-Italian xenomanes.

I write all this with the calm of a determined patriot, I who have been much applauded abroad, and have had more jeers than cheers in Italy, and nonetheless give thanks every day to the cosmic powers that gave me the high honour of being born Italian.'

F.T. MARINETTI

the great
futurist
banquets

Marinetti and guests at a Futurist banquet.

The chef and the staff at the Holy Palate Restaurant

the holy palate
restaurant

The manifesto of Futurist cooking stimulated many discussions and meetings of chefs and restaurateurs. Some were hostile, some enthusiastic. From among the latter, for his keenness to transform food and atmosphere, the painter Fillìa and the architect Diulgheroff picked out Angelo Giachino, the proprietor of a Turin restaurant, whose very customers were urging him to create new-style dishes.

At the close of the Turin Poetry Competition, surrounded by Futurist paintings from the Codebò Gallery, Marinetti, having crowned with the aluminium helmet the Champion poet of Turin, Tullio d'Albisola, baptized with the name of HOLY PALATE the restaurant destined to be first to develop Futurist cooking.

While the restaurant was being decorated, Ercole Moggi, one of the most brilliant Italian journalists, announced what was projected in a leading article over two columns in the *Gazzetta del Popolo* of 21st January 1931.

'A communication to the Roman press from the painter Fillìa, Vice-Secretary General of the Italian Futurist Movement, has set the gastronomes of the capital buzzing, including those journalists particularly attached to the 'Holy Sister Happiness' school of good cooking, to the traditions of the 'spaghetti lover' and to all the other proud insignia of the true epicure. Within the Futurist movement Fillìa is as it were the Lieutenant-General of the action squad. He is not content with planting the seeds of Platonic ideas, but tries to see they are well-set, always husbanding and harvesting them personally. Of course he also garners a few cabbage heads, potatoes and other vegetables, but also applause, agreement and encouragement.

The partisans of pasta hoped that the Manifesto of Futurist Cooking would remain simply theoretical, either polemical argument or literary rhetoric. They obviously don't know these dear boys! The Futurists are now in fact giving warning of a powerful offensive against the old ways of cooking, with a practical and original idea: the opening of an experimental Futurist kitchen in Turin which will be called the 'The Holy Palate Restaurant', and where new dishes will not just be studied Futuristically but presented to the public. So Turin, in one leap, comes closer to being the cradle of another Italian risorgimento: the gastronomic one.

Special trains to Turin

An authoritative Roman paper, commenting half-seriously and half-facetiously on the Futurists' announcement, writes:

'We are sure that the State Railways will offer 50% reductions so that all Italians can travel to Turin en masse to taste the famous 'sculpted meat' in the 'Holy Palate Restaurant'.

Fillìa is perhaps the most dynamic of the Italian Futurists. One should describe him in a Futurist way: call him, I don't know, - a saucepan always on the boil, a 200HP engine, a nitro-glycerine bomb, an erupting volcano ...

He obviously loves Turin because he has always tried out his major ideas there.

'Holy Palate'
no speculative investment

We managed to get hold of Fillìa and not let him go. There were too many important statements waiting to exit from that volcanic brain. Here is what Fillìa said to me:

'First of all, please make it plain that our initiative and actions in opening the 'Holy Palate' have only the artistic, creative and energizing aims of a culinary theory of ours. There is no question of any financial speculation by Diulgheroff or myself. We will simply give the restaurant a Futurist identity. But, I repeat, we will not have any investment in the success of the enterprise, whether great or small (we hope it will be very great). The restaurant will open very soon in Turin. It will be decorated by the architect Diulgheroff and myself with the precise aim of putting Futurist theory into practice.'

'Readers must know that Fillìa is the inventor of the 'sculpted meat' which is the new Futurist dish most widely discussed today in Italy and abroad; so much so that − according to rumour − Prof. Donati in the interests of scientific investigation has offered to give a free laparotomy to the first tasters of 'sculpted meat'.'

As they say, the proof of the pudding is in the eating ...

The reader will ask what on earth 'sculpted meat' is. Here is the authorized description:

'The meat sculpture, a symbolic interpretation of Italian regions, is composed of a large cylindrical rissole of minced veal, stuffed with eleven different kinds of cooked green vegetables and roasted. This cylinder standing upright in the centre of the plate, is crowned with a layer of honey and supported at the base by a ring of sausages resting on three golden spheres of chicken meat.'

Nourishment by radio

So Fillìa will be directing the renewal of Italian cooking in 'The Holy Palate' in Turin, and realizing and presenting the new dishes of Futurist artists and chefs. The tavern will not be a simple, ordinary restaurant but will take on the character of an arts centre holding competitions and organizing Futurist poetry evenings, art exhibitions and fashion shows instead of the usual post-prandial coffee evenings or dances.

'The Holy Palate' will shortly announce its precise technical programme. Among the most important points to note are the following which I reproduce verbatim:

a) 'The Futurists, by declaring themselves against pasta and indicating new developments in Italian cooking, are not only assisting the important goal of national savings, but intend to change the tastes and eating habits of the Italians. Therefore it is not just a question of replacing pasta with rice, or of preferring one dish to another, but of inventing new foods. Many mechanical and scientific changes have come into effect in the practical life of mankind that it is also possible to achieve culinary perfection and to organize various tastes, smells and functions, something which until yesterday would have seemed absurd because the general conditions of existence were also different. We must, by continually varying types of food and their combinations, kill off the old, deeply-rooted habits of the palate; and prepare men for future chemical foodstuffs; we may even prepare mankind for the not too distant possibility of broadcasting nourishing waves over the radio.'

This first point needs no comment. It's a complete revolution. Up till now in certain restaurants there was such a smell – God forbid! Now we will be reorganizing smells. For example, the smell of washed plates will be transformed into the scent of lavender.

The really miraculous idea, which may even have escaped Marconi, is the possibility of broadcasting nutritious radio waves. After all, the notion is not so extraordinary. Since the radio can diffuse asphyxiating and sleep-inducing waves (lectures, jazz, poetry readings, to-conclude-ladies-and-gentlemen, etc.) it surely should be able to diffuse some extracts from the best dinners and luncheons. Then what abundance there would be! The trouble is, that would lead to the abolition of cooking and thus of 'The Holy Palate'.

The second point is abundantly clear:

b) Until now, except for desserts, cooking has not paid much attention to the aesthetic side. Today our refined sensibility requires a complete 'artistic' study of cooking. We must fight against puddles of sauce, disordered heaps of food, and above all, against flabby, anti-virile pastasciutta. We will create meals rich in different qualities, in which for each person dishes will be designed which take into account sex, character, profession and sensibility.

Marinetti
will officially open 'The holy palate'

Fillìa then told me some other important things. It is not true that the Futurists are enemies of wine and meat. Fillìa said:

'Our next announcement about 'The Holy Palate' will make it very clear that until such time as chemistry creates synthetic substances which have the strengths of meat and wine, we must defend meat and wine against every attack. The Manifesto of Futurist cooking has nothing in common, therefore, with the statements of Marco Ramperti, but tends rather towards new culinary horizons to restore taste and enthusiasm to eating, to invent dishes that induce happiness and optimism and multiply infinitely the joy of living: this is something we cannot possibly get from the dishes we have the 'habit' of eating.'

Another important thing which I learned is that Futurist food will not be expensive. A dinner at 'The Holy Palate' will be normally priced.

I asked the Vice-Secretary of the Futurist Movement if the opening of 'The Holy Palate' would be a ceremonial affair. He replied:

– 'Certainly, because it is a very important occasion. The eyes of the world are upon us. Even Academician Marinetti will take part in the opening and answer any criticisms.'

This is certainly a useful new idea. Until now in a restaurant the poor consumer has never found anyone who would answer for a nasty meal. At 'The Holy Palate' we'll have a member of the Academy. And he'll respond in rhyme.

– Can you give us an idea of the menu for the Inaugural Dinner?

– It will include a few dishes that I have devised such as: *Totalrice* (with rice, salad, wine and beer); the famous *Sculpted Meat*, the Meal-in-the-Air (tactile, with noises and aromas); the *Elasticake*. Besides these it will include the architect Diulgheroff's advertising dishes and simultaneous foods by Marinetti and Prampolini. The desserts will be *Networks in the Sky* by the sculptor Mino Rosso and *Ultravirile* by the art critic and Futurist cook P.A. Saladin. Added to this menu will be perfumes, music, surprises, originality, all kinds of unexpected things to create the proper atmosphere for a new kind of meal.

It is clear that it could not be anything but an extraordinary success, the music, perfumes and other surprises aside. The invention of the dish 'ultravirile'

68

would be enough to make Doctor Woronoff weep with envy.

    — 'And what will be left of the old cuisine?' I asked Fillìa.

    He replied in an inexorable tone:

    — 'Nothing, not even the old saucepans. Artusi's day is over. We will be hard.'

    I felt two tears run down my cheeks. So it's farewell, then, to tagliatelle with ham, delight of my ravenous youth. Please, Fillìa, be merciful: at least spare our old Romagna salami, that venerated succulent salami which, together with the blonde Albana, fired the poetic inspiration of Giosuè Carducci and Giovanni Pascoli.'

This article, reproduced in all the newspapers, unleashed a flood of mocking and ironic comments on the digestive values of Futurist foods. It is impossible even to list the best writings of that period. The painter Fillìa, replying to various attacks, repeatedly clarified the importance of the opening of 'The Holy Palate' in the Genoa 'Lavoro', in the Cremona 'Regime Fascista', and the Rome 'Tribuna'. We reproduce, in part, his reply to a Roman chef who threatened Futurist cooks with thunderbolts from the Italian Academy of Gastronomy.

'... the expostulations of the academic cooks strangely recall the opposition that Professors of Art History have always raised to movements of artistic renewal in this century and the last. We are sure therefore that the prophecies of the illustrious Member of the Culinary Academy will have the same result as the others: that is, that they will hasten our success.'

'... criticizing the dishes discussed in the manifesto of Futurist cooking is not just a matter of talking about 'technique': those dishes such as my sculpted meat which was erroneously thought to have been created in opposition to pasta, are the first examples in a whole series we will create. Hence we will have inexpensive dishes and more luxurious ones — dishes which will come out better in a comparison with pasta and others that will win any competition with the old delicacies. And, as for technique, without a doubt the Futurist restaurant in Turin will triumph over the science of the academic cooks. But, in any case, it is the revolutionary spirit of the manifesto which really counts: that is, the urgent need to change our cooking because our whole way of life has changed and because, as it breaks old habits, the palate must be prepared for the foods of the Future. If the academic cooks challenge us purely on reasons of technique, they are beaten; their opposition as artisans cannot win against our strength as artists. And the Futurist creations will achieve technical perfection, while the old dishes, albeit technically perfect, will not be capable of renewal.'

'The Holy Palate Restaurant, decorated by the architect Diulgheroff and myself, will generate an atmosphere which will be a summary of our modern mechanical life and so it will be 'necessary' to serve new and consequently Futurist dishes.'

'... according to the comfortable pacifist theory of the academic cooks not even pasta was ever invented: and we continue to eat as the ancient Romans did. But we live at a moment when everything must be renewed. In the same way that new ways of dressing, new means of transport, new arts, etc., etc., have emerged, Futurist cooking will also come to triumph. Apart from anything, famous doctors and wise cooks acknowledge we are right and support our struggle.'

'The Holy Palate Restaurant has a proprietor and chefs who will run it. The architect Diulgheroff and I are only involved in opening it and setting it on its initial course: we can rely on the intelligence and fidelity to modernity which inspires those chefs. But if the National Academy of Gastronomy insists on frustrating our efforts to invent a truly Italian cuisine, then we will found a Futurist Academy of Gastronomy to which the fifty thousand innovating artists and sympathizers of the New Italy will belong.'

Even before its official opening, The Holy Palate Restaurant in Turin achieved world fame because it publicly announced the realization of Futurist cuisine. Meanwhile the building works proceeded and the interior was designed predominantly in Italian aluminium from 'Guinzio and Rossi'. This material was intended to give the place a metallic, shining, elastic, light and serene atmosphere; to give it the sense of how we live today, with our minds and bodies needing to find the correlative, the synthesis, and the artistic translation of the mechanical organization which prevails. Aluminium is the most suitable and expressive material for creating this atmosphere, it has these essential qualities and is truly a child of this century, deserving eternal glory on a par with the 'noble' materials of the past. In the Holy Palate Restaurant then, a shimmering aluminium structure was designed which, far from being coldly deployed to fill space, served as a working element of the interior: dominant aluminum, the supple bone structure of a new body, completed by the rhythms of indirect lighting. Light is undoubtedly one of the fundamental realities of modern architecture and must be 'space', must play a living role along with other forms of construction. Within the aluminium body, then, light served as an arterial system, indispensable to the surrounding organism in a state of activity. Everything conspired to complete the interior: the giant publicity pictures, the hangings, the decorative glass and sundry objects.

One of a set of dishes for a 'Life of Marinetti' cycle designed by Giuseppe Mazzotti, 1939.

the first futurist dinner

The Holy Palate Restaurant was officially opened on the evening of the 8th March 1931 after a feverish day of intense labour in the kitchen, where the Futurists Fillìa and P.A. Saladin competed with the restaurant's chefs, Piccinelli and Burdese, to prepare the dishes. Here is the list of dishes for the first Futurist dinner:

1. *Intuitive Antipasto (formula by Mrs Colombo-Fillìa)*
2. *Sunshine Soup (formula Piccinetti)*
3. *Totalrice with wine and beer (formula Fillìa)*
4. *Aerofood, tactile, with sounds and smells (formula Fillìa)*
5. *Ultravirile (formula P.A. Saladin)*
6. *Sculpted Meat (formula Fillìa)*
7. *Edible Landscape (formula Giachino)*
8. *Italian Sea (formula Fillìa)*
9. *Mediterranean Salad (formula Burdese)*
10. *Chickenfiat (formula Diulgheroff)*
11. *Equator + North Pole (formula Prampolini)*
12. *Elasticake (formula Fillìa)*
13. *Network in the Sky (formula Mino Rosso)*
14. *Fruits of Italy (simultaneous composition)*
Wines by Costa − Beers by Metzger − Spumanti by Cora − Perfumes by Dory.

Here without further delay is a description of the evening as it appeared in the newspaper 'La Stampa' in a comprehensive article by the staff writer Dr. Stradella:

'No one can be unaware of the interest and controversy awakened throughout the world by the coming official opening of *The Holy Palate*. The event will assume an exceptional importance because of this and the date remain impressed in the history of the art of cooking, just as the dates of the discovery of America, the storming of the Bastille, the Congress of Vienna or the Treaty of Versailles are indelibly fixed in the history of the world.'

An announcement couched in these terms cannot but be itself exquisitely Futurist. To be fair we must acknowledge that the Futurists are loyal to the principles of their doctrine to the last limits and beyond. 'While recognizing,' warns Marinetti, 'that great deeds have been performed in the past by men badly or crudely nourished, we affirm this truth: that we think, dream and act according to what we eat and drink.'

Towards food in pills

Not content with the extraordinary victories in the worlds of painting, literature and the arts generally, which have accumulated over the past twenty years, Italian Futurism aims today at fundamental change; in fact it dares once again to face unpopularity, with a programme of total renewal in our way of eating.

We forgot to say that *The Holy Palate*, notwithstanding its slightly blasphemous appearance to a vulgar passéist, is a delicious Turin restaurant where, yesterday evening, the first Futurist dinner was held: a parade of fourteen different dishes, various wines, perfumes, spumanti.

Our readers, or perhaps better, our gentle lady readers, will basically want to know the most recondite reasons behind this attempted creation, to speak in passéist terms, or behind this complete achievement, to speak Futuristically. The request is legitimate; and anyway to comply with it helps pin down the exact nature of the responsibility we feel we have to respond. But whatever the case, we shall respond scientifically, with precision, making use of the very words of the Head of the Italian Futurists: 'It is our automatic practice as Futurists to ignore traditional models and authority in order to create, at any cost, a *new* way of thinking, which everyone considers *crazy*, but which will henceforth establish the proper nourishment for a faster and ever more airborne life.'

Many foods are being abolished in consequence: at the head of the list, pasta; meanwhile we wait for chemistry to complete its specific task, that is 'to give the body the calories it needs as quickly as possible, utilizing equivalent nutrients (provided free by the State) in the form of powder or pills'; this is a unique idea, designed to achieve 'a real lowering of the cost of living and of salaries, with a relative reduction in working hours'. We will wait for that day, mean

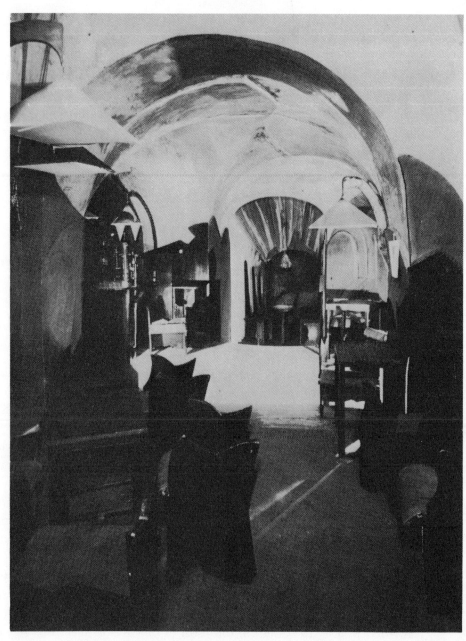

Interior of a Futurist cabaret and exhibition space designed by Anton Giulio Bragaglia (1923).

The Futurist restaurant, The Holy Palate, 2 Via Vanchiglia, Torino, redesigned by Fillìa and Diulgheroff. The first Futurist banquet was held here 8th March, 1931.

Marinetti and one of his cooks.

while it will be possible to create perfect meals, depending on an original harmony between the setting (crystal, china, table decoration) and the flavours and colours of the foods and absolute originality in the dishes themselves.

In the aluminium restaurant

But now let's go back to *The Holy Palate Restaurant*, created, designed and decorated by the architect Diulgheroff and the painter Fillìa, and which you have to imagine as a huge cube-shaped box grafted along one side on to another smaller one: the box is adorned with entirely luminous, semi-colourless columns and large metallic eyes, also luminous, embedded halfway up the wall; and this, finally, is covered with the purest aluminium from the ceiling to the floor. Here, towards midnight on Sunday, the Turin Futurists and their guests were invited to gather. To lead the ceremony were present, amongst others, Academician Marinetti, Felice Casorati, the painter Peluzzi, the painter Vellan, the sculptor Alloati, Prof. Guerresi, a few journalists and many lovely ladies in deliciously passéist *toilettes*.

The official *Speaker*, in other words the announcer and illustrator of each individual course, was and could only have been the painter Fillìa. As we said there were fourteen different dishes. This is what they were. First: *Intuitive Antipasto*. It's not difficult to grasp that here in one sense it was a question of a surprise, and in another sense, of a preparation for the meal ahead. At this point we must not forget that the invention of appetizing food sculptures whose original harmony of form and colour feeds the eyes and excites the imagination before tempting the lips is a fundamental rule for a perfect meal. Therefore let's choose a large orange, and making a tunnel inside, relieve it of its pulp: we will then carve the fleshless shell into the shape of a little basket, with a handle and a round cavity. Into this we will place a little piece of breadstick and thread on it a small slice of ham, an artichoke heart soaked in oil and a pickled chili pepper. Into the lap of these things it will then be appropriate to slip a tiny rolled up piece of paper on which has been inscribed a Futurist maxim or a eulogy of one of the guests. It will be easy to find this *surprise* thanks to the decreed 'abolition of knives and forks for food sculptures, which can give prelabial tactile pleasure.' In sum, a very fine thing.

A dish
with sounds and scents

Second: *Aerofood*, tactile, with sounds and scents (devised by Fillìa). Here there are a few little complications. Eating futuristically, one uses all the five senses: touch, taste, smell, sight and hearing. We put to the reader a few other rules for the perfect dinner which will help us to enjoy fully the taste of all the courses to come: first the use of the art of perfumes to enhance the gastronomic experience. Every dish will thus be preceded by a perfume attuned to it, which will be dispelled from the table by electric fans. Next the use in measured doses of poetry and music as unexpected ingredients to accentuate with their sensual intensity the flavours of a given dish. The second course consists of four parts: on a plate are served one quarter of a fennel bulb, an olive, a candied fruit and a tactile device. The diner eats the olive, then the candied fruit, then the fennel. Contemporaneously, he delicately passes the tips of the index and middle fingers of his left hand over the rectangular device, made of a swatch of red damask, a little square of black velvet and a tiny piece of sandpaper. From some carefully hidden melodious source comes the sound of part of a Wagnerian opera, and, simultaneously, the nimblest and most graceful of the waiters sprays the air with perfume. Astonishing results: test them and see.

The flavour of steel

Third course: *Sunshine soup* (created by the chef Ernesto Piccinelli). This is a *consommé* in which a few sun-coloured ingredients are cradled. Excellent. Fourth course: *Totalrice* (by Fillìa). This is a very simple thing: a risotto, Italian style, seasoned with beer, wine and fondue. Exquisite.

Fifth course: *Sculpted Meat*. This dish is a milestone in Futurist cooking. For the delectation of our lady readers we will transcribe the recipe: 'a symbolic interpretation of all the varied landscapes of Italy, it is composed of a large cylindrical rissole of minced roast veal, stuffed with eleven different kinds of cooked green vegetables and roasted. This cylinder, standing upright in the centre of the plate, is crowned by a layer of honey and supported at the base by a ring of sausages resting on three golden spheres of chicken meat.' A marvel of balance.

Sixth: *Utravirile*. We will not dwell on minute details: suffice to say that this is a dish designed for the ladies.

Seventh: *Edible Landscape*. This is the reverse of the preceding dish; it is only for the gentlemen. Highly enjoyable.

The *Italian Sea, Mediterranean Salad* and *Chickenfiat*, the eighth, ninth and tenth dishes are served at the same time. Note particularly the last named dish, devised by Diulgheroff. One takes a good-sized chicken and cooks it in two stages: first boiled, then roasted. A capacious cavity is dug out of the shoulder of the bird, within which one places a handful of little ballbearings made of mild steel. On to the rear part of the bird one sews in three slices a raw cockscomb. The sculpture thus prepared goes into the oven for about ten minutes. When the flesh has fully absorbed the flavour of the mild steel balls, the chicken is served with a garnish of whipped cream.

Two dishes were then served which were not included in the programme. One of them, offered only to the journalists, was not very easy for us to decipher. We thought we tasted hints of Bologna mortadella sausage, mayonnaise and that sort of Turin caramel known as pasta Gianduia; but 24 hours after eating it, after a careful examination of our consciences, we don't believe we can say for sure. The other unlisted dish, however, which the painter Fillìa called *Porroniana* and Marinetti: The Excited Pig, was simpler. An ordinary cooked salami is served immersed in a concentrated solution of strong black coffee and flavoured with eau-de-Cologne.

And so the ceremonial dinner came to an end. Over the spumante the speakers were Felice Casorati, the sculptor Alloatti, the lawyer Porrone, Emilio Zanzi, the painter Peluzzi and finally Academician Marinetti, who vividly praised Fillìa and Diulgheroff for the concrete results they had achieved.'

Contemporaneously there appeared: in the 'Gazzetta del Popolo' an amusing article by Ercole Moggi, *The Futurist Holy Palate restaurant inaugurated by F.T. Marinetti*; in 'Regime Fascista' an enthusiastic report by Luigi Pralavorio: *Pasta is dead: long live Sculpted Meat*; and in the 'Giornale di Genova' a favourable article by Marcaraf, *The Ceremonial Opening of the Holy Palate Restaurant*. These journalists were present at the dinner. Later Moggi's and Stradella's articles were reprinted in all the Italian and foreign papers, with vociferous comment and many photographs depicting the restaurant premises, the form of the dishes, etc. etc.

As more journalists and photographers arrived from Rome and Paris at 'The Holy Palate Restaurant', Ercole Moggi, after a further interview with the painter Fillìa, published another article in the 'Gazzetta del Popolo': *The Mysteries of Futurist Cooking Revealed*, in which were given the exact formulae for the first realized dishes, an indication of the minimum cost of Futurist dinners and an announcement of other surprising events imminent. Beneath the headlines 'Futurist Cooks Put To The Test' – 'This Is Nothing, We're Going Much Further' – 'Fillìa versus Artusi' - 'Holy Palate? Holy Smoke!', the biggest daily newspapers in the world spread the word, discussed it and argued over it. From Stockholm to New York, from Paris to Alexandria in Egypt, whole pages of illustrated papers appeared dedicated to the argument. Futurist cooking had succeeded in imposing itself and thus began the most intense period of its campaign to renew alimentary habits.

●

Discussions about Futurist Cooking were not limited only to the gastronomic sphere, because our desire for renewal has always been expressed clearly in favour of all branches and all activities of art and life. The support of various journalists, builders, architects, etc., who in line with our battle speak of the need to change restaurant interiors, to breathe modernity into agricultural and industrial fairs, and thus to present the foods and produce of our cities and farms in the spirit of our times, must be emphasized.

In the Manifesto of Futurist Cooking we speak very precisely of the need to make use of electricity and of all machines that can improve the work of cooks. Many restaurants adopt electric kitchens, electric ovens, etc., but unfortunately they go abroad for them, forgetting that in Italy unrivalled manufacturers exist of kitchens, ovens, water heaters, etc., etc. The engineer Pittaluga, for instance, recently brought to our attention the intense propaganda by the State Electricity Board for Italian products and pointed out how unfortunate it was that the proprietors of large restaurants were still shy of these machines, which not only offer the best guarantees, but are from time to time revised according to their function and application, to their indisputable advantage compared with foreign imports.

In another field, it is worth noting the article by Dr. Alamanno Guercini, Editor-in-Chief of the 'Giornale Vinicolo Italiano' (who has dealt intelligently with Futurist Cooking in many articles), which takes up the problem of the design of public places where Italian wines and other drinks are consumed. Here are the most significant points from his article:

'There are many people in this world who love old architectural forms and enjoy modern wine (prepared in ultramodern oenological establishments!) within medieval walls or strangely complicated catacombs resonant with the basically primitive music of a 'jazz band'. These people don't take into account that in those remote times the grape was trodden by feet; or if they do they attach no importance to it. Probably they don't wish to remember that the wooden casks, which greatly add to the decor around them are – alas! – diminishing in importance in the new cellars which have gone over floor after floor to enormous batteries of multi-storey reinforced cement containers.

For example: in a recently built establishment near Rome, with a capacity of 40,000 hectolitres, only 15,000 are reserved for wooden barrels.

Even the poor barrels, under the influence of modernism, trying to make themselves as oval as possible, have exploded in the construction of enormous 800-hectolitre vats.

We must overcome our personal artistic predilections and champion more utilitarian and economically practical ways of advertizing wine in these modern times.

With respect to all opinions, it seems to me that wine today could well look for and find in the art of innovators, in the genius of the Futurists, a very valuable alliance wherever architecture, décor, trade exhibitions, restaurants, presentations and publicity are concerned.

Wine may be a drink of very ancient tradition, but it is also a drink which renews itself annually, modernizes itself in a multitude of progressive ways; it is a dynamic drink, which fuels the man and the engine.

This is not to negate or criticize all the other artistic attempts to show the advantage of wine; but only to ask that the doors be opened to avant-garde artists and to their artistic and publicistic activities, which for many reasons are likely to prove very acceptable to a wide public of producers, industrialists, businessmen and consumers.

The organizers of trade fairs and exhibitions will be able to do a great deal.

In the regular competitions at their trade exhibitions, viticulturalists, before building *stands*, before organizing publicity, ought seriously to consider making use of exciting new artistic ideas.

It's time to extol and advertize wine according to modern and Futurist criteria applied in a practical way.

In Paris at the Colonial Exhibition many of the pavilions for tasting wine, beers, liqueurs, and those offering restaurant meals, specialities etc. were in the rational style. And the most modern and the most animated was the Italian restaurant conceived by the Futurist architects Fiorini and Prampolini.

In Paris, Berlin and Vienna hundreds of *bars* are in the Futurist style. In them is hygiene, economy, light, space and the splendour of metal and glass.

In Padua the Pavilion of Religious Art is a truly useful rational creation, beautiful and in keeping with its function.

Many catalogues for French wines are totally Futurist in design.

And to the many merits of modern restaurants, Futurist catalogues and Futurist posters may be added economy: not something to be sneezed at in these difficult times.

In Italy, until now, experiments along these lines have been few and far between; yet these Italian artists' work is greatly appreciated abroad.

I would like to hope that in 1932, if the wine trade holds any exhibitions in Rome, they will take full advantage of the new forms of art.

There should be room for everyone in the field of publicizing wine!

And if the Italian Futurists can play a productive and practical role in advertizing and promoting Italian wine, they will be doing something useful and good.

This is what I hoped for a year ago, when I wrote about Futurist Cooking in the 'Giornale Vinicolo Italiano'.

And now we invite these innovatory artists to collaborate with us with the intention of serving the viticultural interests of the nation in the same way.'

culinary lectures

The debate about Futurist cooking roused such intense feeling in everyone that all of Marinetti's lectures were immediately followed by noisy arguments for and against pasta, for and against the new Futurist foods.

Marinetti, in front of enormous crowds, gave the following lectures between February 1931 and February 1932, in which he extolled and brought to public attention the virtues of the new way of eating.

'Salle de L'Effort' in Paris, officially opening the Exhibition of Futurist Aeropainting.

'The Vitelli Gallery' in Genoa, at the opening of the exhibition of the avant-garde and Futurist group 'Synthesis'.

'The Botti Gallery' in Florence, during the Exhibition of Futurist Aeropainting

'The Artists' Circle' in Trieste, opening the exhibition of Futurist Aeropainting.

'The Novara Friends of Art', inaugurating an Exhibition of works by the Futurist painters Fillìa, Oriani, Mino Rosso, Diulgheroff, Pozzo, Zucco, Saladin, Alimandi and Vignazia.

'The Social Circle' in Cuneo, at the opening of one-man shows by the Futurist painters Fillìa and Zucco.

'The Fascist Institutes of Culture' in Brescia and Cremona.

A propaganda tour to various cities in Tunisia.

Futurist lectures in Budapest.

'The National Theatre' in Savona, on the occasion of the Exhibition by the Turin and Ligurian Futurist groups.

Lectures in Sofia and Istanbul.

the futurist dinner
in novara

During the 'Futurist Art Exhibition' at the Circle of the Friends of Art in Novara, Dr. Rosina, President of the Federation of Businessmen, arranged a banquet under the direction of the Futurists Fillìa and Ermanno Libani. The latter, as the editor of the newspaper 'L'Italia Giovane', described the event in a witty article:

'It really is a pity that at the Futurist supper held on Sunday 18th April in Novara no one took down in shorthand for the future the comments with which Fillìa announced each dish.

The bill of fare was composed of the following novelties: *Intuitive antipasto; aerofood (tactile with sounds and scents); totalrice; sculpted meat; Italian sea; chickenfiat; elasticake; simultaneous fruit;* Italian wines, beer, spumanti, perfumes and music.

The time set for sitting down at table had already passed and no one said anything about getting this Lucullan feast underway. I got up to ...

– Look, my dear friend, in being late even you are passéists; I thought the Futurists, if only to do something new, would have started early but instead there's the usual boring wait just like at all the banquets in this bourgeois world.

He looks at me and smiles ironically – to eat in the future ... what's more Futurist than that?

the start of the dinner

God willing, the God of the Futurists that is, the God Fillìa will present at the exhibition of sacred art in Padua, we sit down at table: *Intuitive Antipasto*. There is a general conviction that this dish will be a real leap in the dark to keep faith with its definition as intuitive: but no. We are served with very elegant little baskets carved out of oranges and full of what constituted the old antipasto dear to our great-grandmothers: salami made from real pork and some Cirio pickles, all transfixed by little bits of breadsticks which, historians of this sort of thing inform us, were already being used twenty years ago.

But actually there is something new and it consists of tiny pieces of paper hidden inside the stuffed olives. The idea is to spit it out, open it and read it out loud to the great delight of those listening: Emanuelli is the greatest journalist, signed Enrico Emanuelli.

But this too was nothing new.

the aerofood

We come now to the *aerofood*: it is a dish I would not recommend for the hungry. It is composed of a slice of fennel, an olive and a kumquat. In addition there is a strip of cardboard on which are glued, one next to the other, a piece of velvet, a piece of silk and a piece of sandpaper: the sandpaper — Fillìa explains — need not be eaten, it is only there to finger with the right hand and provide prelabial sensations which make the food much more tasty as contemporaneously the left hand tries to bring it to the mouth.

As for the scents, the waiter goes round with a large spray can dousing the heads of the diners (we suggest to Fillìa that another time they serve these capillary ablutions tepid to avoid the calamity of bald men catching cold).

The dinner, with many jokes and witticisms, proceeds joyously: what has put everyone into such a good humour is the announcement that there will be no official speeches. The rather roguish Grignolino wine is also a little to blame.

And good digestion is safeguarded.

Totalrice: a very virile dish in shape and composed basically of rice seasoned with wine and beer. Very edible: there are even some who ask for a second helping.

After the *totalrice* a change of scene: the white lights go out and the red ones remain lit: semi-darkness. The Cavaliere Fontana whispers in my ear: Futurist food, like verses by certain modern poets and like man-made brilliants, needs lots of half-shadow.

Next will come a dish invented out of thin air by the Cavaliere Coppo, owner of the Albergo d'Italia.

The waiters serve it while a *battistangola* reproduces the sound of frogs croaking.

Rice and beans, frogs and salami.

The best.

But why haven't they reproduced the grunting of the pigs too? — someone asks. After all there's a lot of salami!!

The *sculpted meat* — shouts Fillìa — is the product of all the gardens of Italy.

Here one does run the risk of getting indigestion!

We move on to the *Italian sea*, which even passéists could easily introduce into the roll-call of family favourites.

Fillets of fish cooked in butter are laid out along the length of an oval plate and fixed to them in descending order, with the help of toothpicks, are a candied cherry, a piece of Australian banana and a piece of fig.

On the two sides of the plate creamed spinach and at top and bottom Cirio sauce. It looks like a travesty of a transatlantic liner, but it tastes like our best cooking.

As a form of protest I am keeping silent about the *chickenfiat*. To calm us down Fillìa eulogizes the woman of the future — bald with spectacles. And I must say they'll make a perfect combination: bald women and *chickenfiat*!

The *elasticake* is made from modest puff pastry, filled with cream in violent colours. It is an elastic sweet because on top of each cream puff we have stuck a piece of prune.

The *simultaneous fruit* is composed of various pieces ... of peeled fruit connected to each other: orange, apple, dried fruit.

Coffee, stop.

the great
futurist banquet
in paris

At The Colonial Exhibition in Paris the Futurist architect Fiorini came up with an audacious design for the pavilion which was to be the site of the Italian restaurant. The interior of the Pavilion, a huge room with more than 100 tables, had been brilliantly decorated with 8 enormous panels by the Futurist painter Enrico Prampolini: these panels, it was generally recognized, represented everything most modern, lyrical and inventive that could be imagined in the theme 'colonial'. This gave the place an atmosphere simultaneously African and mechanical, which was a splendid rendering of the wish to interpret colonial motifs according to a modern and Futurist sensibility.

In this eminently suitable setting, the publishers 'Edizioni Franco-Latini' represented by Signora Belloni, Signorina Farina and Signor Pequillo wanted to create Futurist food for the first time in Paris and they agreed with the painters Prampolini and Fillìa on preparations for a dinner.

The crowd which thronged on the eve of the show to take part in the great Futurist banquet was the cream of Paris society. The major French newspapers were represented.

The *lista delle vivande:*

1. *Les grandes eaux (du peintre Prampolini).*
2. *Carrousel d'alcool (du peintre Prampolini).*
3. *Hors d'oeuvre simultané (du peintre Fillìa).*
4. *Excitant gastrique (du peintre Ciuffo).*
5. *Préface variée (du peintre Prampolini).*
6. *Toutriz (du peintre Fillìa).*
7. *Les îles alimentaires (du peintre Fillìa).*
8. *Equator + Polo-Nord (du peintre Prampolini).*
9. *Aéromets, tactile, bruitiste et parfumé (du peintre Fillìa).*
   Poulet d'acier – à surprise (du peintre Diulgheroff).
Cochon excité – à surprise (d'un primitif du 2000).
10. *Viandesculptée (du peintre Fillìa).*

11. *Machine à goûter (du peintre Prampolini).*
12. *Paradoxe printanier (du peintre Prampolini).*
13. *Gateauélastique (du peintre Fillìa).*
14. *Vins – Mousseux – Parfums – Musiques – Bruits et chansons d'Italie.*

In addition, between courses dances, songs and musical numbers were announced.

The Futurist journalist Francesco Monarchi, editor-in-chief of *La Nuova Italia* described the banquet like this:

'The events that we are about to disclose are of an exceptional gravity. In fact the simple announcement of a Futurist banquet had aroused among 'bien-pensant' compatriots a wave of disapprobation and hostility which then portended to a mass spiritual boycott. These 'right thinkers' found the revolutionary character of the planned new dishes which had been announced outrageous because according to them traditions, especially gastronomic traditions, are sacrosanct.

For the record let us acknowledge that the names of the dishes could indeed give rise to the gloomiest apprehensions and the complications of the music, perfumes, tactile settings, noises and songs constituted an additional a fear which was difficult to overcome.

Despite this wave of pessimism many courageous people braved the distance, the inclement weather and the terror of what lay ahead to crowd into the Futurist pavilion last Wednesday evening.

●

At the entrance Signora Belloni and Signorina Farina, organizers with *Edizioni Franco-Latine* of the evening, welcomed the heroic guests. Utterly pale with emotion (a pallor which, however, only added to their grace), the two ladies took on the absolutely impossible task of encouraging the fearful who, having reached the threshold, in a last paroxysm of doubt did not dare enter the room.

However, the cheerful festivity of the surroundings enlivened by Prampolini's enormous panels, the electrifying self-confidence of Academician Marinetti, the imposing battery of waiters and the traditional white calm of the laid tables returned to the hesitant the courage of their convictions.

Only the enigmatic faces of the creators of the Futurist foods, Prampolini and Fillìa, maintained the mystery of the imminent ceremony.

Contrary to our usual habit, we will give a full list of names, since they will go down in history as the first to taste the food of the future.

His Excellency the Prince of Scalea, always ready to respond to any Italian event, was at the table of honour with a few members of his commissariat, amongst whom the Commendatore Dall'Oppio and the Marquess of San Germano, with the representative of Minister Reynaud, the Regent of the Fascio Doctor Saini, the Rt. Hon. Ciarlantini, the lawyer De Martino, Administrative Secretary of the Fascio, the Cavaliere Gennari of the Directory.

At other tables: the lawyer Gheraldi of the Society of Authors, Vittorio Podrecca, the art critic Eugenio d'Ors of the Academy of Madrid, Count Emmanuele Sarmiento. Doctor Lakowsky, Signor Cartello, the noted painter Sepo, Signor Pequillo of *Edizioni Franco-Latini*, etc.

Many ladies, elegant ladies too, had boldly entrusted themselves to the adventure. We observed: the Marchioness of San Germano, Madame Van Dongen, Countess De Fels, Madame Mola, Madame De Flandreysy, Madame Lakowsky, Signora Podrecca, Madame Madika, Madame Tohaika, Miss Moos, Madame Massenet-Kousnezoff, Signorina Cirul, Madame Ny-eff, Madame Castella, Signora Pequillo, Signorina Budy, Durio, etc.

At 9:30 a formidable striking of the gong brings the guests face to face with reality. An unexpected green light makes the diners appear even more spectral.

The two aperitif mixtures created by the painter Prampolini are announced:

'The Great Waters' and 'Alcoholic Carousel'. General surprise to find in one of them chocolate and cheese floating in Barbera, citron syrup and bitters, and to fish out from the other a white capsule containing a mouthful of anchovies. A few grimaces, but a first result satisfying enough for several people to have seconds.

Three first courses served contemporaneously cut short discussion of the aperitifs. Fillìa's 'simultaneous antipasto' (chopped apple peel, salami and anchovies), and Prampolini's 'tummy tickler' (a disc of pineapple with sardine, tuna and nuts) and 'varied beginning' (butter, olive, tomatoes and tiny sugar-coated sweets), if they cause alarm with their audacious combinations, quickly make friends with the palate.

No respite: Fillìa's 'Totalrice' is announced as a medley of rice, beer, wine, eggs and Parmesan cheese. It is devoured by the diners who begin to tone down their primitive state of mind.

First interval: Signorina Jole Bertacchini, from the San Carlo in Naples, sings delightfully and is much applauded.

Inexorably the impressive parade of waiters starts again, bringing in this time Fillìa's 'Edible Islands', an exquisite union of fish, banana, cherry, fig, eggs, tomato and spinach.

Another interruption: Mila Cirul begins her dances which arouse enormous and sustained excitement. In fact this exceptional dancer's very modern art is difficult to surpass, for perhaps she alone has grasped how much beauty may derive from an absolutely new and brilliant interpretation of dance.

As people began to get a little used to Futurist food, Count Sarmiento, who had offered to introduce the courses, announced the painter Fillìa's Aerofood.

The 'Aerofood' is composed of different fruits and vegetables which are eaten with the right hand, without the help of any cutlery, while the left hand caresses a tactile surface made of sandpaper, velvet and silk. Meanwhile the orchestra plays a noisy, wild jazz and the waiters spray the napes of the diners' necks with a strong perfume of carnations. The room resounds with the shrieks of the ladies violently doused with perfume, with general hilarity and firm and interminable applause. (Only one person seemed left out of the surrounding enthusiasm: immediately asked why, it turned out she was left-handed — so she had stroked the tactile surface with her right hand while she ate with her left.)

By now the Futurist food revolution had triumphed. Fillìa's *Sculpted Meat*, Prampolini's *North Pole + Equator*, his *Paradox of Springtime* and *Tasting Machine*, Fillìa's *Elasticake*, despite the audacity of their shapes and original-ity of their contents, were much appreciated.

Among the different courses, two surprise dishes were reserved for just ten persons. The *'Steel Chicken'* by Diulgheroff and *'The Excited Pig'*. The body of the chicken mechanized by aluminium-coloured bonbons, and the salami immersed in a sauce of coffee and eau-de-Cologne, were declared excellent.

Another interval: Signora Maria Kousnezoff, from the Opera and the former Imperial Theatre of Petrograd, showed once again, in two songs accompanied on the piano by maestro Balbis, the exceptional vocal qualities which have made her famous throughout the world.

Signor Roberto Marino, from the Monte-Carlo Opera, then gave a marvellous rendering of some Neopolitan songs.

●

Academician Marinetti, who took part in the banquet, not only presiding over it but joining in at every moment to discuss and exalt the food, praised the Futurist dinner as the first fulfilment in Paris of the ideals of the famous manifesto of Futurist cooking, a manifesto which aroused worldwide debate, with more than 2000 articles, and demonstrated the art-life symbiosis which has always been the motive force behind Futurism.

After praising the gastronomic creations of the painters Prampolini and Fillìa and commending the magnificent organization of the evening by 'Edizioni Franco-Latine', Academician Marinetti with his usual fresh eloquence paid homage to the courage of those present and noted with satisfaction the general sense of well-being.

Academician Marinetti, with great vivacity, came then to the songs and dances, pointing out the desired contrast between the lyrical part of the evening (exclusively traditional) and the thoroughgoing Futurism of the dinner and the dances.

●

Before the applause for Marinetti's brief and vital speech had died away, Josephine Baker appeared in the room, accompanied by Signor Abbatino.

La Baker was given a wildly enthusiastic welcome and stayed until the closing moments of this exceptional party, which ended with some very animated dancing.

Josephine Baker, having immediately become the all consuming and vital centre of attention, played a very important part in the successful outcome of the party: her fascinating presence helped in the final conquest of any lingering doubts among the guests about the consequences of Futurist cooking.

the futurist aerobanquet in chiavari

The Commendatore Tapparelli organized a marvellous Futurist Day in Chiavari on 22 November 1931, during which a Futurist Art Exhibition was opened, a Poetry Competition held (won by the Trieste poet Sanzin) and a lecture was given by F.T. Marinetti on *'World Futurism'*. In addition, more than three hundred people took part in a great aerobanquet held at the Hotel Negrino; the most important officials of the city and province were there.

Long articles were written about the occasion in all the Ligurian newspapers, in the *Corriere della Sera*, and many other Italian papers. We reproduce here the essential points of a light-hearted article in the *Corriere Mercantile* by a staff writer:

'The highlight of the day – at least for the reporter intent on diversion and hungry, as the cliche would have it, for local colour – was undoubtedly the 'First Futurist Aerobanquet', a kind of food sculptural orgy which took place in the great rooms of the Hotel Negrino and put the stomachs of a good three hundred guests to quite a test.

Every dish was scrupulously prepared by the famous cook Bulgheroni who had come specially to Chiavari from Milan to break down with his appetizing creations the massive closed door of ravioli and pastasciutta.

Some surprising dates

The meal, beyond the wildest expectations of those present, many of whom felt a churning in their gastric cavities which could not be put down entirely to appetite but to understandable fear, began with a *Timbale of Tomorrow*: a sort of appetizer perhaps too poetic to be appreciated by the needs of the stomach, which as everyone knows, is a crude materialist. This timbale was composed of the head of a newborn calf, miserable and disconcerted, in the middle of a superabundance of pineapples, nuts and dates: these dates once bitten into revealed themselves pregnant with an almost Cyclopean surprise: they were, in fact, carefully stuffed with anchovies so that out of this innocent head, out of these pineapples and African fruits with the added complexity

of fish, a sort of pudding was born that left every esophagus choked with
admiration.

Roses in the soup

We proceeded then impetuously to *Taste Buds Take Off*: a name indicating
a soup of fairly bizarre nature, composed in almost equal parts of concentrated meat stock, *champagne* and liqueurs: on top of this mixture, which for
initiates is said to have extraordinary appetitive qualities, floated some large
rose petals, graceful and fragile. Confronted with such a masterpiece of bro-
thy lyricism the guests courageously tried the experiment of swallowing; but
more than one, with obvious aversion, forebore to continue to the end and
contented himself with just taking a rose petal from the bowl, drying it with
his napkin and placing it inside his wallet as a souvenir of the meal and evi-
dence of a banquet of which he would later tell his grandchildren.

The third course, the Ox in the Cockpit, consisted of some very mysterious
meat balls over whose composition it is neither good nor helpful to speculate,
placed on top of aeroplanes made of bread. The planes were fine, the meat
balls less so. However this dish was among the most appreciated, being one
which offered many of the guests the chance to still their hunger with bread
which had never before appeared to be such a divine and precious food.

Candied atmospheric electricities

And now the waiters appear with great trays bearing the Vegetal Flight Booster
consisting of a discreetly diabolical mixture in which slices of beetroot and
slices of orange nestled together, united by oil and vinegar and a little pinch
of salt. By this time many of the diners had already put their digestive systems
into a not quite normal condition, so they could not really be blamed for being
unable to repress an instinctive gesture of terror when the tray carrying the
'conclusive foods' appeared. These foods gloried in the extremely dynamic
name of '*Candied Atmospheric Electricities*'. These dear and unforgettable
'electricities' looked like little brightly-coloured bars of marbled soap, containing
a sweetish cream made from ingredients that only an exhaustive chemical
analysis would be able to define. I have to say, with a journalist's scruple,

that only a very few of the banqueters dared to put these bars of soap into their mouths: unfortunately I don't know the names of those daring souls. I say unfortunately because a cluster of heroes like these deserves, at the very least, eternalization in bronze.

And so we arrived at the *Landing on Water Digestive*: a landing that not everyone managed to carry out, since a good number had already sunk at the moment of takeoff. Marinetti rose to speak and with a marvellous eloquence which sprang from him so spontaneously it was as if he had not touched food he launched into an outburst worthy of a Public Prosecutor against the infamy of pasta and the ignominy of ravioli, exalting Futurist dishes by contrast, particularly those amphibious dates we were able to taste so memorably at the beginning of the banquet.

After Marinetti sat down the poet Farfa jumped to his feet and declaimed with aviatorial impetuosity a quasi-Pindaric ode entitled Song of the Tubers.

the futurist aerobanquet in bologna

The Futurist painters Caviglioni and Alberti organized an important exhibition of Aeropainting at the Journalists' Circle in Bologna, which was officially opened by F.T. Marinetti on 12th December 1931. Afterwards the same painters, amidst much anticipatory excitement, prepared a great Aerobanquet in the Casa del Fascio (which cost 20 lire a head). It is described thus in the *Resto del Carlino*:

'Public interest in the Aerobanquet was enormous and the hall of the Casa del Fascio, especially chosen for this extraordinary gastronomic experiment, yesterday evening at 9:30 (even the hour was slightly unusual!) welcomed a huge crowd amongst whom could be distinguished celebrities and officials, painters, journalists, ladies and bon viveurs. Among the dignitaries were the Prefect of the Province, the Commendatore Turchi and the Rector of the University Prof. Ghigi, who had come to sanction with the sacred seal of Academe the seditious movement against pasta.

Marinetti in his study, 1938.

As if in an aeroplane

The Aerobanquet was able to live up to its name because of the mis-en-scène designed by the organizers. The tables were arranged sloping at various angles, giving the impression of an aeroplane. There are the wings — slender and narrow like those in a high-speed hydrofoil — and the fuselage, and at the far end the tailpiece (empty, as they usually are in real planes). Between the wings a huge propeller — not turning, fortunately! — and behind it two motor-cycle cylinders, promoted for the occasion to the rank of aeroplane engines.

In place of the usual tablecloths we find sheets of silver paper, which in the organizers' imagination pretend to be aluminium, and a shiny tin plate functioning as a place setting, in which the ladies may check — oh, fancy chancing on such a delightful mirror! — their compromised *maquillage*.

The synthesism of the table is obvious. There is very little to see on it. The glasses are the usual ones, the plates and cutlery ditto; but there are no flowers at all and they are replaced by ... raw potatoes, brightly-coloured and artistically carved; and woe betide those who cannot distinguish between things which serve to please the stomach and those destined to delight the eyes. Another real novelty: the bread. No ordinary rolls or French loaves or Viennese *kipfel*, but cleverly-fashioned rolls in the form of monoplanes and propellers; and I must confess that the shapes led most excellently to a perfectly baked dough and crust.

Final component: the waiters wear blue celluloid collars, while the painter Alberti, organizer of the meal, sports a pompous and very flashy Depero waistcoat in a thousand colours.

Risotto with oranges

The Aerobanquet opens in lightly passéist fashion: with an appetizer. It's called 'Piquant Airport', but resembles nothing so much as a Russian salad *alten-styl*, with the addition of a slice of orange married to a slice of hard-boiled egg and an olive. And the orange is spread with butter coloured pink ...

However, before opinions on the first dish can be expressed, dish number two majestically advances to the 'ohs and ahs!' of the company.

The *menu* calls it 'The Roar of Ascent' but Academician Marinetti rebaptizes the dish 'Orange Risotto', in which the rice is still the rice ... of days gone by, but the sauce — oh, the sauce! — is based on oranges. And slices of fried orange gild the blanket whiteness of the dish.

The orange risotto, we are bound to say, provokes a little unrest in the ranks.

... and the 'nutritious' noises

We fear the advent of some complications, when suddenly the room is immersed in a diaphanous blue light and an engine starts up in the room next door. The painter Alberti gravely announces — but why does that man smile? — that the plane is flying at a height of 8000 metres, and Marinetti authoritatively confirms this, explaining:

— Observe how the sound of the engine rouses and nourishes the stomach ... it is a kind of massage of the appetite ...

Finally we re-descend from the culinary 'stratosphere' and the crowd can find nothing better to do than start to beat furiously on their tin plates, promoting them to the role of 'noise intoners'.

We want the national fuel!

And the national fuel (*vinum vulgaris* from our hillsides) advances triumphantly, decanted from a few tins labelled Extrathick Oil. And the wine is in drums. The wine is in jerry cans ... , and while they wait for the central dish the diners eagerly nibble the wings of the bread aeroplanes.

But then the central dish arrives — the 'sculpted meat with veal fuselage'. And it is an indisputable success. To be truthful, the dish is Futurist only in its allusions. What it consists of, in fact, is a veal escalope, allied to a large thin sausage, and the vegetables are two little onions and two fried chestnuts. But after the experiment based on oranges, two chestnuts flanking a sausage no longer create an impression!

A pity that the meat — after the usual tour round the table to be shown off — arrives barely warm. And it doesn't help that Academician Marinetti does nothing against ... the cold, saying that at 8000 metres food can't stay hot ...

A little later the Futurist chief turns on the pacific Dr. Magli, representing the learned society of the Achaei, reproaching him for daring to criticize the meat before tasting it.

– That – he exclaims – is passéist. There's no valour in it ...

Magli bounces back:

– Very true ... I should have held it to my ear to hear if it was nutritious.

– And Homeric laughter greets his witty reply.

And so the Aerobanquet flies on from dish to dish amidst exchange of wit, glasses of national fuel, and a nostalgic *sottovoce* reference to tortellini. Academician Marinetti, however, has no nostalgia. (He would like us not to have any either.) He is so enthusiastic about the symposium that he asks the cooks to come before him to be applauded. But having been called they are slow to come, and Marinetti has to repeat himself. Bring out the cooks. – And then a stentorian voice is heard from the back of the room, shouting:

– They're not coming because they're afraid of us!

But this was obviously a calumny, because immediately afterwards, two *cordons bleus* from the Casa del Fascio make their entrance, to be greeted with applause from Marinetti and his followers. But the two cooks are uncertain. They fear being made fun of and having almost lost their voices seem to be saying:

– Forgive us, gentlemen, for we ourselves are not to blame ...

Down with the 'museum-kitchen'

Having begun with an appetizer, the banquet closed with some speeches. First the Gold medalist Onida rose to speak, then Dr. Magli expressed the feelings of the 'tagliatellists', while someone sent an anonymous telegram, the text of which said: 'Ok, down with pasta, but tagliatelli is another kettle of fish!'.

Finally Academician Marinetti rose to declare that his eloquence was literally choked by the rich and delicious variety of aerofoods we had tasted, some of which – he added – were very important discoveries, such as the rice flavoured with oranges. He then wove a eulogy of Futurist cuisine, in comparison with which pasta was definitely in retreat.

Tagliatelli – he says – is the passéists' last stand; the last stand of egg pasta. Futurist food is the realization of the general desire to renew our eating habits and of the fight against weight, big bellies, obesity. We need to maintain the vitality we Italians had in our youth in Antiquity, and in our early manhood in the Middle Ages, even if the years mark us with their storms and fogs. The militarization of a young culture is where we find our strength. Therefore we do not want Italian cooking to remain a museum. We affirm that Italian genius can invent another 3000 dishes, equally good, but more in keeping with the changed sensibility and changed needs of the contemporary generation.

With a new round of applause for his colleagues from Bologna, Academician Marinetti concluded his speech and the Aerobanquet came to an end, while the diners took away as souvenirs the tin plates on which the Futurist chief had been constrained to sign his name using the point of a fork as a burin.

typical anecdotes

Besides the thousands of articles which discussed, exalted, derided, condemned and defended the great Futurist banquets in Turin, Novara, Paris, Chiavari and Bologna, an enormous number of caricatures and anecdotes circulated in all the weeklies, the illustrated magazines and directly amongst the public. Several volumes would have to be compiled to collect together all the enormous explosion of zany thoughts, ideas and jokes suggested by Futurist cooking in theory and practice.

The following anecdotes are typical:

1) In Aquila, an incalculable number of women united to sign a solemn petition in favour of pastasciutta. This petition was addressed to Marinetti. The women of Aquila, who had never agitated before about anything so important, felt this collective rising to be necessary, so deeply ingrained was their faith in pastasciutta.

2) A Genoese newspaper printed the announcement of the founding of a society called P.I.P.A (International Pasta Propaganda Association) which held various competitions to combat the hated food and to invent new ones.

3) In Naples people marched in the streets in favour of pasta.

4) In San Francisco, California, the clients of two Italian restaurants, one on the ground floor and one on the first floor of the same building, came to blows for and against Futurist food and there ensued a riotous battle from the windows and in the street with edible projectiles and saucepans. There were a few casualties.

Marinetti and guests at a Futurist banquet.

5) In Turin the most famous chefs held a conference to decide on the merits of Futurist cooking which ended in violent arguments between the two sides.

6) In Bologna, in the midst of a great student dinner, F.T. Marinetti arrived and, to everyone's astonishment, avidly ate a plate of spaghetti: only afterwards did the diners realize that Marinetti was just a fellow student very cleverly disguised.

7) Photographs of Marinetti in the act of eating pasta appeared in a few mass-circulation magazines: they were photographic montages carried out by experts hostile to Futurist cuisine, who were trying to discredit the campaign for a new way of eating.

8) A theatrical magazine was published in Bologna entitled 'Sculpted Meat'.

9) In Turin, an operetta by Sparacino and Dall'Argine was produced entitled 'The Holy Palate'.

In the meantime while all the arguments were bouncing back and forth, a new sense of optimism and joy triumphed over the nostalgic, grey habits of old-style dining and the Futurists, surpassing their first creations, developed further original inventions.

A page from 'Les mots en liberté futuristes'.

the definitive futurist dinners

It is not only that Futurist Cooking proposes a complete revolution in the nourishment of our race, with the aim of making it more joyful, spiritual and dynamic. Futurist Cooking also proposes, through the art of harmoniously combining Futurist dishes, to evoke and provoke essential states of mind which cannot otherwise be evoked or provoked.

We have put together some dinner programmes that we call PROVOCATIVE AND EVOCATIVE.

heroic winter dinner

A group of soldiers who at three o'clock on a January afternoon will have to get into a lorry to enter the line of fire at four, or go up in an aeroplane to bomb cities or counter-attack enemy flights, would seek in vain the perfect preparation for these in the grieving kiss of a mother, of a wife, of children or in re-reading passionate letters.

A dreamy walk is equally inappropriate. So is the reading of an amusing book.

Instead these fighters sit down round a table, where they are served a 'Drum Roll of Colonial Fish' and some 'Raw Meat Torn by Trumpet Blasts'.

DRUM ROLL OF COLONIAL FISH: poached mullet marinated for twenty-four hours in a sauce of milk, rosolio liqueur, capers and red pepper. Just before serving the fish, open it and stuff it with date jam interspersed with discs of banana and slices of pineapple. It will then be eaten to a continuous rolling of drums.

RAW MEAT TORN BY TRUMPET BLASTS: cut a perfect cube of beef. Pass an electric current through it, then marinate it for twenty-four hours in a mixture of rum, cognac and white vermouth. Remove it from the mixture and serve on a bed of red pepper, black pepper and snow. Each mouthful is to be chewed carefully for one minute, and each mouthful is divided from the next by vehement blasts on the trumpet blown by the eater himself.

When it is time for the *Peralzarsi;* the soldiers are served plates of ripe persimmons, pomegranates and blood oranges. While these disappear into their mouths, some very sweet perfumes of roses, jasmine, honeysuckle and acacia flowers will be sprayed around the room, the nostalgic and decadent sweetness of which will be roughly rejected by the soldiers who rush like lightning to put their gas masks on.

The moment they are about to leave they swallow the Throat-Explosion, a solid liquid consisting of a pellet of Parmesan cheese steeped in Marsala.

Formula by the Futurist Aeropoet
MARINETTI

Marinetti at a Futurist banquet in Tunis.

summer luncheon
for painters and sculptors

After a long period of rest, a painter or sculptor who wants to take up his creative activities again at three o'clock on a summer afternoon may vainly try to excite his artistic inspiration with a succulent – traditional meal.

Weighed down, he would then have to walk to digest it and beset by cerebral anxieties and pessimism would end up wasting the whole day loitering artistically without creating any art.

Instead a meal may be served to him made up of pure gastronomic elements: a bowl of good tomato soup, a big yellow polenta, a heap of green salad, not dressed and not on a plate, a bowl full of olive oil, a bowl full of strong vinegar, a bowl full of honey, a big bunch of red radishes, a mass of white roses complete with thorny stems.

As the spirit moves him, without plates or cutlery, and continually refusing to follow the usual nervous habits which crop up, he assuages his hunger while looking at Umberto Boccioni's picture of 'The Football Player'.

Formula by the Futurist Aeropoet
MARINETTI

springtime meal
of the word in liberty

Walking across a spring garden through the gentle flames of a dawn full of childish timidity has plunged three young men dressed in white wool, without jackets, into a state of literary and erotic anxiety that cannot be appeased by a normal meal.

They sit down at a table out of doors under an arbor that allows the warm fingers of the sun to pass through.

They are immediately served with a synoptic-syngustatory plate, not hot, but gently warmed, of peppers, garlic, rose petals, bicarbonate of soda, peeled bananas and cod liver oil equidistant from each other.

Will they eat it all? Will they taste just parts of it? Will they grasp the imaginative relationships without tasting anything? It's up to them.

Next they dutifully eat a bowl of traditional clear soup with tortellini. This has the effect of making their palates take flight quickly to search on the synoptic-syngustatory plate for an indispensable new harmony.

Instantly they make an unusual metaphorical connection between the peppers (symbol of rustic strength) and the cod liver oil (symbol of ferocious northern seas and the need to cure sick lungs) so they try dipping the peppers in the oil. Then each clove of garlic is carefully wrapped in rose petals by the same hands of the three guests, who thus entertain themselves with the coupling of poetry and prose. The bicarbonate of soda is available for use as the verb in the infinitive of all food and digestive problems.

But tedium and monotony can arise after the tastebuds have savoured the garlic and roses. So then a buxom country girl in her twenties enters, holding in her arms a huge bowl of strawberries floating in well-sweetened Grignolino wine. The young men invite her with high-flown words-in-liberty devoid of all logic and directly expressing their nervous condition, to serve them as quickly as possible. She serves them by tipping it over their heads. They end up eating, licking, drinking, mopping themselves up, fighting each other across the table with illuminating adjectives, verbs shut between full stops, abstract noises and animal cries which seduce all the beasts of springtime, as they ruminate, snore, grumble, whistle, bray and chirrup in turn.

Formula by the Futurist Aeropoet
MARINETTI

autumn musical dinner

In a hunter's cabin secluded in a green-blue-gilded forest, two couples sit down at a rough table made from trunks of oak.

The brief blood-red twilight lies in agony beneath the enormous bellies of darkness as if under rain-soaked and seemingly liquid whales.

As they wait for the peasant woman to cook, the only food that passes along the still empty table is the whistle that the wind makes through the door lock, to the left of the diners.

Duelling with that whistle is the long, sharp wail of a violin note escaping from the room on the right belonging to the peasant woman's convalescent son.

Then, silence for a moment. Then, two minutes of chick peas in oil and vinegar. Then, seven capers. Then twenty-five liqueur cherries. Then twelve fried potato chips. Then a silence of a quarter of an hour during which the mouths continue to chew the vacuum. Then, a sip of Barolo wine held in the mouth for one minute. Then a roast quail for each of the guests to look at and inhale deeply the smell of without eating. Then four long handshakes to the peasant woman cook and off they all go into the darkness-wind-rain of the forest.

Formula by the Futurist Aeropoet
MARINETTI

nocturnal
love feast

A terrace in Capri. August. The moon pours a stream of curdled milk straight down on the tablecloth. The brown-skinned, heavy-breasted native mama enters carrying with an enormous ham on a tray and speaks to the two lovers who are lying stretched out in the two deck chairs, uncertain if they should renew the fatigues of the bed or begin those of the table:

— 'This is a ham that contains a hundred different pork meats. In order to sweeten it and free it from any possible bitterness and virulence I have soaked it for a week in milk. Real milk, not that illusory milk of the moon. Eat as much of it as you like.'

The two lovers devour half the ham. Large oysters follow, each with eleven drops of Muscat wine from Syracuse mixed into its sea water.

Then a glass of Asti Spumante. Then the *War-in-Bed*. The bed, vast and already full of moonlight, fascinated, comes to meet them from the back of the open room. They get into it, toasting each other and sipping from the War-in-Bed. It is composed of pineapple juice, egg, cocoa, caviare, almond paste, a pinch of red pepper, a pinch of nutmeg and a whole clove, all liquidized in Strega liqueur.

Formula by the Futurist Aeropoet
MARINETTI

Marinetti and his wife Benedetta in their apartment in Rome.

tourist dinner

(Created for the travelling Futurist Exhibition Paris – London – Brussels – Berlin – Sofia – Istanbul – Athens – Milan).

List of foods:

1. *Pré-salé aux petits pois, surrounded by saffron risotto.*
2. *Roast-beef surrounded by freshwater shellfish and Halva.*
3. *Sausages floating in beer, dusted with crystallized pistachios.*
4. *Strawberry juice to be drunk on pancakes fried in oil.*
5. *Alternate wells of honey and wells of Roman Castelli wine on a flat square of mashed potatoes.*
6. *Peaches stoned and filled with sweet Tuscan wine and closed up again, floating in a sea of cognac.*
7. *Marinated eel stuffed with frozen Milanese minestrone and dates which themselves have been stuffed with anchovies.*

Formula by the Futurist Aeropoet
MARINETTI

official dinner

The Futurist Official dinner avoids the grave defects that pollute all official banquets:

FIRST: the embarrassed silence stemming from the fact that there is no pre-existing harmony between the table companions.
SECOND: the conversational reserve, owed to diplomatic etiquette.
THIRD: the moroseness produced by insoluble world problems.
FOURTH: the rancour of frontiers.
FIFTH: the low, wan, funereal and banal tone of the dishes.

In the Official Futurist Dinner, which should take place in a large hall decorated with enormous panels by Fortunato Depero, after a rapid distribution of *polibibite* and *traidue*, there takes the floor, without getting up, the Sganciatore, a guest who does not belong to any diplomatic corps or political party, but is chosen from among the most intelligent young parasites of the aristocracy and noted for his total recall of obscene jokes.

The Sganaciatore, guided by whatever level of moroseness he must overcome, will immediately tell, in a low voice, three very obscene jokes but without himself descending to vulgarity. Once laughter amongst the diners has sparked a line of fire from one head to the next, a sloppy soup of tapioca and milk will be served in a monastery tureen to ridicule and put to flight all diplomacy and reserve. Then follow:
1) 'The Cannibals sign up at Geneva': a plate of various raw meats from which the guests cut what they want, seasoning the pieces by dipping them into little bowls of oil, vinegar, honey, red pepper, ginger, sugar, butter, saffron risotto or old Barolo wine.
2) 'The League of Nations': little black salami sausages and tiny pastries filled with chocolate custard, floating in a cream of milk, eggs and vanilla. (While this dish is being tasted, a twelve-year-old Negro boy, hidden under the table, will tickle the ladies' legs and pinch their ankles.)
3) 'The Solid Treaty': a multi-coloured castle of nougat with, inside, very tiny nitro-glycerine bombs which explode now and then perfuming the room with the typical smell of battle.

When it is time for the dessert, the Organizer of the official dinner will enter and with many ceremonious excuses, beg the diners to await the arrival, continually promised but invariably delayed by complications, disasters on the road and train derailments, of a paradisical fruit picked on the Equator, and an ice cream so fantastically architectural it has disobligingly just collapsed in the kitchen.

The comments, wisecracks and catcalls which greet the Organizer's excuses will have scarcely faded away before the same fellow is back again at the door repeating his excuses. This goes on for half an hour.

Then there enters, instead of the miraculous fruit, a familiar old drunk dredged up from the depths that very night and brought by force into the official banquet.

Logically he demands more to drink. A choice of the best Italian wines, of great quality and quantity, is lavished on him, but on one condition: that he speak for two hours on possible solutions to the problem of disarmament, the revision of treaties and the financial crisis.

Formula by the Futurist Aeropoet
MARINETTI

wedding banquet

The usual wedding banquet beneath its seeming and ostentatious air of festivity hides a thousand preoccupations: will the couple be happy or not — intellectually, sexually, prolifically, professionally, economically?

Everyone proffers good wishes the way they launch rockets, with fear in the tips of their fingers and tongues.

The mother-in-law feverishly disburses compliments, advice, compassionate looks and glances of false joy. The virgin is already in the arms of the angels. The husband-to-be, well groomed, is well oiled. The cousins all vinegar and pickle. The girlfriends of the bride all brushes, combs and pins of envy.

The kids stuff themselves with nuptial sweets and tumble about crushing the orange blossoms on their wedding outfits.

No one can eat or taste the food, as they are all feeling wobbly and the stabilizing of their palates and stomachs is repugnant to them.

Therefore the prevailing mood of the dinner is a balancing act which corresponds to their tightrope states of mind.

A tureen of magnificent soup, known and loved by all (rice, chicken livers and beans in quail broth) is borne aloft on three fingers by the cook himself, hopping on his left leg. Will he reach the table or not? Perhaps he will topple over, in which case the stains on the wedding dress will be a good chance to correct its insolent and uneventful excessive whiteness.

Next scene is the cleaning up, with everyone helping. The groom remains calm: it is he who, having gone out for an instant, comes back with a tray, laden with Milanese saffron risotto and an abundance of truffles the colour of sin, balanced on his head. If this dish tips over too, and turns the wedding dress as yellow as an African sand dune, it will also be so much time gained by an unexpected shortening of the voyage.

Some sautéed mushrooms are served next, pompously praised by the usual maniacal huntsman:

— 'I gathered them all myself, between bagging a partridge and a hare in the Pistoia woods, drenched with rain. There's every kind of mushroom, except the poisonous ones … unless my myopia has played an ugly trick on me. At any rate, they're so beautifully cooked I would say be brave and tuck in.

For my part I shan't hesitate, though I fear a few absolutely fatal ones lurk somewhere in there.'

Naturally a heroic contest begins.

They're so good, says the bride.

— 'You're not afraid, darling?'

— 'I'm less afraid of them than of the infidelities you're likely to commit, you brute!'

Then, a little over-hastily, the joker customary to every wedding party begins to howl, holding his stomach. Is he pretending to suffer or is he really tortured by pains of mysterious distant or nearby origins?

It doesn't matter much. Everyone laughs. Lots of people eat the mushrooms. The cook, entering in a fury, hands in his notice, mortally stricken by the suspicions rather than by the mushrooms, which are absoloooooooootely innocent, absoloooooooootely sound.

Next there's a Fernet for everyone. But still under the eloquence of the huntsman, hares and partridges are served cooked in spiced wine. He himself has concocted this dish in the kitchen with the pounded flesh of other well-hung partridges mixed with old Robiola cheese in rum. A huntsman's delight.

Dazzled by his words, inebriated by the Soave-sweet perfume of the Soave sewer, the guests eat copiously, washing the food down with Barbera and Barolo.

The huntsman begins to speak again:

- 'Among all these partridges, the fattest, that .one there, gave me a ten kilometre chase. From one end of the valley to the other, I finally had to go right down to the bottom, to the river, and climb up again. I would recognize its beautiful red feathers every time. Now it's finally stopped, or rather it still seems to be alive, actually I think it's still moving.'

— 'It's moving because it's crawling with worms,' shouts a wag.

A long freeze seems to paralyze the diners, substituting for the usual ice cream which as it happens is bad for stomachs which have become so heated in the acrobatic juggling of happiness, alarming mushrooms and dynamic partridges.

Formula by the Futurist Aeropoet
MARINETTI

economical dinner

1) 'The Total Rustic': apples cooked in the oven, then stuffed with beans which have been boiled in a sea of milk.

2) 'Country Crime': aubergines cooked in tomatoes, then stuffed with anchovies and served on a bed formed half and half of spinach puree and lentil puree.

3) 'City Peppers': big red peppers, each enclosing a *poltiglia* of cooked apples in a pocket of sugared lettuce leaves.

4) 'Flooded Forest at Twilight': endives cooked in wine, strewn with boiled and sugared beans.

This dinner is eaten while a talented reciter of poetry makes the National Poet Farfa's humorous lyrics resonate explosively by imitating their typical voice of a short-sighted exhaust pipe.

Formula by the Futurist Aeropoet
MARINETTI

the bachelor dinner

Futurist cooking sets out to avoid the usual pitfalls of eating alone:

1) The anti-human solitude that fatally drains a part of the stomach's vital forces.

2) The heavy silence of meditative thought which taints the food and makes it leaden.

3) The lack of a living, human, fleshy presence, which is indispensable for keeping alive the palate of the man who is confined to the zone of animal flesh.

4) The inevitable speeding-up of the rhythm of the jaws as they take flight from boredom.

In a dining room decorated with Aeropaintings and aerosculpture by the Futurists Tato, Benedetto, Dottori and Mino Rosso, on a table whose four legs are made of accordions, some food portraits are presented on jingling plates bordered with bells:

1) 'Blonde Food Portrait': a beautiful piece of sculpted roast veal with two long eyes of garlic in a dishevelment of chopped boiled cabbage and small green lettuces. Dangling earrings of little red radishes soaked in honey.

2) 'Dark Man-Friend Food Portrait': well modelled cheeks of pastry — moustache and hair of chocolate — big eyes of milk and honey with pupils of liquorice. A split pomegranate for the mouth. A nice necktie of tripe in broth.

3) 'Beautiful Nude Food Portrait': in a small crystal bowl full of fresh milk, two boiled capon thighs, the whole scattered with violets.

4) 'Food Portrait of the Enemies': seven cubes of Cremona nougat, each one with a little well of vinegar on top and a big bell hanging on one side.

Formula by the Futurist Aeropoet
MARINETTI

extremist banquet

For this banquet, where no one eats, and the only satiety comes from perfumes, the guest may stay at the table for two days. The banquet will take place in a villa constructed for the purpose by Prampolini (to a design by Marinetti), on a tongue of land dividing the most lakelike of lakes — slow, lazy, deserted, stagnant, — from the widest and most marine of seas.

There are French windows, which open electrically by means of a keyboard placed under the guests' fingers: the first opens on to the mass of smells from the lake, the second on to the mass of smells from a barn and its associated storehouse of fruit, the third on to the mass of odours from the sea and its associated fishmarket and the fourth on to a hothouse and its carousel of rare, odoriferous plants gliding past on tracks.

It is an evening in August. The perfumes of the surrounding countryside are at their maximum intensity but are kept out by closed windows, like the lock gates on a canal.

The eleven guests (five women, five men and a neuter) each have a little electric fan which they can use at will to drive each scent, once enjoyed, away towards the corner where there is a powerful suction fan. Before the banquet begins the guests recite 'Eulogy of Autumn' by the Futurist poet Settimelli and 'Interview with a Billy-Goat' by the Futurist poet Mario Carli.

Along the length of the table in the shape of a parallelepiped things spring into view and glide along like cars, appearing and disappearing:

1) a food sculpture equipped with a vaporizer and which looks and smells like a castle of Milanese risotto, washed by a sea of spinach with wave crests in cream.

2) a food sculpture equipped with a vaporizer and which looks and smells like a ship made of fried aubergines sprinkled with vanilla, acacia flowers and red pepper.

3) a food sculpture equipped with a vaporizer and which looks and smells like a lake of chocolate surrounding a little island of peppers stuffed with date jam.

The three vaporizing food sculptures suddenly stop moving when three kitchen boys wearing white silk and tall shiny white hats burst into the room shouting:

— 'You are the bosses, but you're rascals too! Are you or are you not going to eat these exquisite dishes which we great artists have prepared for you? Stop all this mumbling or we'll boot you!'

The neuter trembles like a hopeful seismograph. Off they go.

A noisy, long, loud ringing for five minutes.

A pause. But the silence yields to the invading polychattering and croaking of the frogs in the lake that accompanies the slow opening of the French windows, intensified by the odours of waterlogged grasses and old burnt reeds, giving off traces of ammonia and a whiff of phenic acid. All the guests use their hand fans like shields against the lakeside windows.

Then the windows giving onto the storehouse of fruits are flung open, and four smells (the first of apples, the second of pineapple, the third of muscat grapes and the fourth of carobs) erupt into the room. A whinny escapes from the neuter, but immediately a hundred wriggling, slippery saline seaside smells flood in from the other window bringing visions of immense foaming gulfs and tranquil, fresh green anchorages at dawn.

The neuter recovers:

— 'At least twelve oysters and two fingers of marsala.'

But the order is cancelled at the same time as the sea and all its silver fish, by the powerful scent of roses so curvilinear and succulent that the eleven mouths, left until then thoughtful or astonished, begin feverishly chewing the emptiness.

The neuter whimpers:

— 'For pity's sake, beautiful cooks, bring us something to chew on, otherwise we will see the ugly mouths of these rude men bite into the insipid flesh of our five lady friends.'

— A shudder of fear. Then a stirring and shuffling. The cooks peep in and disappear. The small electric fans cancel everything. A fragrance wafts by — the very delicate, strong, sweet, putrid, hothouse smell of cultivated irises which, coming from the greenhouse, meets an identical perfume, but wild, coming from the lake. The two perfumes of life, flesh, luxury, death synthesize and thus gratify all eleven starving palates.

Formula by the Futurist Aeropoet
MARINETTI

dynamic dinner

In his novel 'The Steel Alcove' F.T. Marinetti describes his anxiety to escape the inevitable dulling of sensibility during dinner:

'On the evening of 1st June 1918, in a bombardiers' hut planted defiantly at an angle on a mountain ridge in the Val d'Astico, we men were eating and drinking happily. The long long red forks of the sunset had intertwined with our forks, and were winding the spaghetti round in a blood red and smoking sky. There were about twenty officers, lieutenants, captains, with Colonel Squilloni, jovial and pompous at the head of the table. Hunger among the bombardiers after a day of hard work. A religious silence of mouths chewing succulent prayers. Heads bent over plates. But the very young men are not fond of silence and want to laugh, to do something. They know my fertile, mischievous imagination and urge me on with glances. There is too much silence at the table and the good doctor is too gravely absorbed in the rite of eating his pasta. With four mouthfuls I placate my stomach; then I jump up and brandishing a forkful of spaghetti, say in a loud voice:

In order not to cloud our sensibilities, company will move two places to the right, quick march!

Then picking up plates, glasses, bread, knife as best I can I give my companion on the right a brutal shove, and he moves over reluctantly, he too picking up everything and giving a shove to the right. The young men carry out the exercise eagerly but the doctor snorts, grumbles, shouts. They relieve him of the burden. The plate of macaroni turns upside down on his jacket. A crash of glasses. Floods of wine. Laughs, yells, uproar. They all push the doctor, tread him like grapes. His cries squirt out.

Taking charge of the rout, I give the order:

— Move accomplished! Everyone sit down! But listen, woe betide anyone who still lets his sensibility grow clouded! ... And you, dear doctor, don't forget that the highest and most precious virtue is elasticity. How could you cure, without elasticity, swollen glands, corns, syphilis, ear infections or stop some of our superiors going soft? Thanks to elasticity we abandoned Karst after Caporetto, we laughed while our hearts cried in retreat. Without elasticity how can we crush Austro-Hungarian passéism and revitalize Italy completely after the victory? I order you, dear doctor, to interrupt your passéist stuffing with Futurist elasticity!

Everyone laughs. The doctor looks at me, frightened. Pretending mockingly to threaten him, I order:

– In order not to dull your sensibility, plates and glasses in hand! Everyone round the table in procession!

There's a hell of a din. Shouts, shoves, 'That's enough!', 'Lay off!', fists, falls, 'For God's sake!' Whirling, rolling, pitching. But the young men are determined and force on the others a wild tour of the table. The Colonel enjoys the bizarre game very much. Only the doctor is not amused. Where is the doctor? Where has he gone? Everyone looks for him. He has fled on to the terrace with his plate of pasta. Come on, come on, to the attack! And the dinner finishes in confusion, disbanded, with a great roar of laughter in the tawny laughter of the sunset, all clouds of incandescent crystal, bottles foaming with gold, heaped-up cirrus clouds of violet porcelain, a luminous aerial banquet suspended on a peak above the twilit Venetian plain.

Around the doctor my friends sing the hymn of Futurist foolery:

Irò irò irò pic pic

Irò irò irò pac pac

Maa - gaa - laa

Maa - gaa - laa

RANRAN ZAAAF

This was the way they murdered nostalgia.'

●

For dynamism therefore we suggest the following foods:

1) 'The Running Step': composed of rice, rum and red pepper.

2) 'In Top Gear': 200 threads of spun sugar wound up in a ball, wrapped in slices of pineapple and drowned in Asti spumante.

3) 'Car Crash': a hemisphere of pressed anchovies joined to a hemisphere of date puree, the whole wrapped up in a large, very thin slice of ham marinated in Marsala.

4) 'Losing a wheel': four thrushes roasted with a great deal of juniper and sage, one with its head missing, wrapped up and rolled into a ball inside a slice of polenta sprayed with Italian eau de Cologne.

5) 'Hand Grenades': a ball of Cremona nougat wrapped in a large, very rare steak, sprinkled with Muscat wine from Syracuse.

The guests, dressed sportively with sleeves rolled up, will gather outside the door of a gymnasium where these balls of food will be set out in little pyramids on the ground.

When the door is open, they all rush forward furiously to the attack, with open mouths and predatory hands. Those who can manage to kick their rivals out of the way will have the best meal, with their chewing mouths and grasping hands. But the most skilful will be the one who, taking his inspiration from Umberto Boccioni's great picture 'The Football Player', manages to grab twenty or so edible balls, leaping out of windows and over balconies and fleeing into the countryside. Mouths, teeth, hands in pursuit. A gastronomic battle finale consisting of open mouths. The players don't bag the foodshot, they eat it.

Formula by the Futurist Aeropoet
MARINETTI
and the Futurist Aeropainter
FILLÌA

architectural dinner
for sant'elia

In honour of the 1931 Poet of National Record Farfa (winner of the 'Sant'Elia' Poetry Circuit) an architectonic dinner was held with a special sensitivity to space. This puts the person being honoured 600 kilometres from those honouring him, but linked to them with telephone wires. The Futurist poets Escodamè, Sanzin, Gerbino, Vittorio Orazi, Krimer, Maino, Pandolfo, Giacomo Giardina, Civello, Bellonzi, Burrasca, Rognoni, Vasari and Soggetti; the painters Dormal, Voltolina and Degiorgio of the Paduan group and the painters Alf Gaudenzi and Verzetti from the 'Synthesis' group of Futurists and Avant-gardeists, gathered together in the directorial offices of the Futurist movement in Rome. To dine they used their hands like children, and alternately built and ate, towers, skyscrapers, battleship guns, airport slipways, belvederes, sports stadiums, military pontoons, elevated railways one after the other:

Three hundred cubes (3 cm high) of pastry. Eight parallelepipeds (10 cm high) of compressed buttered spinach. Ten cylinders (30 cm high) of Cremona nougat. Six balls (15 cm diameter) of Milanese risotto. Five pyramids (40 cm high) of cold minestrone soup. Twenty tubes (1 metre high) of date paste. Five ovoid blocks (20 cm high) of banana paste. Seven screens (60 cm high) of cod cooked in milk.

The Futurists, the better to construct the Futurist house perfected it with their teeth each one sitting on inedible cylinders of compressed pasta.

Formula by the Futurist Aeropoet
MARINETTI
and the Futurist Aeropainter
FILLÌA

aeropictorial dinner
in the cockpit

In the roomy cockpit of a large Autostabilizing DeBernardi, surrounded by Aeropaintings by the Futurists Marasco, Tato, Benedetta, Oriani and Munari which hang from the aeropeaks and clouds on the horizon they are flying over at 1000 metres, the diners free five lobsters intact from their shells and boil them electrically in sea water. They stuff them with a pulp of egg yolk, carrots, thyme, garlic, lemon rind, the eggs and liver of the lobsters, capers. They sprinkle them with curry powder and put them back in their shells, tinted blue here and there with methylene.

Bizarrely the five lobsters are then placed in seeming disorder and at some distance from each other on a huge Tullio d'Albisola aeroceramic, mattressed by twenty different kinds of salad: these being geometrically arranged in a pattern of squares.

And so the diners, holding in their fists little ceramic bell-towers full of Barolo mixed with Asti Spumante, eat villages, farms and fields speeding by.

Formula by the Futurist Aeropoet
MARINETTI
and the Futurist Aeropainter
FILLÌA

aerosculptural dinner
in the cockpit

In the large cockpit of a Trimotor, surrounded by metal aerosculptures by the Futurists Mino Rosso and Thayaht, the diners will prepare a paste of potato flour, little onions, eggs, prawns, pieces of sole, tomato and lobster meat, sponge-cake and chopped biscuits, castor sugar perfumed with vanilla, candied fruits and gruyère cheese, soaked in plenty of Tuscan Vin Santo.

With this they fill eleven moulds (buttered and floured), each one in a shape typical of a mountain, a gorge, a promontory or small island. They will all be cooked electrically.

The eleven pies, removed from their moulds, will be served on a huge tray in the centre of the cockpit, while the diners toss in the air and devour masses of fluffy whipped egg white just as the wind outside plays with the white cirrus and cumulus clouds.

Formula by the Futurist Aeropoet
MARINETTI
and the Futurist Aeropainter
FILLÌA

Marinetti with Prampolini and Tato at the III Roman Biennale, in the Palazzo delle Esposizioni, 1925.

aeropoetic futurist dinner

In the cockpit of a Trimotor flying at 3000 metres in a bipartite sky: the maudlin light of a greenish mother-of-pearl half-moon and a hemisphere of half-clouds lit by long scorpions of gold.

Directly beneath, a river of the most solid silver delivers the estuary of its wriggling eels in a sea of pitch studded with lunar nickel.

From the window on the right: a tinkling of glass wood chaffinches and bells. In the mouth a pellet of honey tastes sour in response. The eyes fly to the left, through the other window, to suck the white aniseed jam that drips slowly from a cloud. In front of the diners, who are three in number, the round altimeter announces: 3000 metres eaten. Near it the tachometer, its dinner companion, announces: 20,000 revolutions devoured. On the other side of the altimeter the speedometer announces: 200 kilometres digested.

The stomach of the human diner seated in the middle corrects with a good many vulgar acids the indigestible excitative power of the abstract poetic suicidal moon liqueur. The mouth of the human diner on the right sucks a tube of yellow red neon gilded by an eternal African summer.

Movement. Lightness. Chewing the infinite. Vertical takeoff. Tilting away from everyday life. The line of artistic power ever ascending. Love hot soft faraway. Hands present but no use. Critical rumble of the intestines. In the mouth of the Futurist Aeropoet a bit more honey from the bees that inspired the Greek poets.

Formula by the Futurist Aeropoet
MARINETTI
and the Futurist Aeropainter
FILLÌA

a tactile dinner party

The host has carefully prepared, with the help of the Futurist painters Depero, Balla, Prampolini and Diulgheroff, as many pairs of pyjamas as there are guests: each pair of pyjamas is made of or covered with a different tactile material such as sponge, cork, sandpaper, felt, aluminium sheeting, bristles, steel wool, cardboard, silk, velvet, etc.

A few minutes before the dinner each guest must put on, in private, one of the pairs of pyjamas. Then they are all brought into a big, dark room empty of furniture: without being able to see, each guest must choose a dinner partner quickly according to his tactile inspiration.

Once the choice has been made everyone comes into the dining room which has been furnished with the right number of little tables for two: surprise at discovering who one has chosen as a partner by the very refined touch of fingers on tactile materials.

The following menu is served:

1. 'Polyrhythmic salad': the waiters approach the tables carrying for each guest a box with a crank on the left side and, fixed half way up the right side, a china bowl. In the bowl: undressed lettuce leaves, dates and grapes. Without the help of cutlery, each diner uses his right hand to feed himself from the bowl while he turns the crank with his left. The box thus emits musical rhythms: and the waiters dance slowly with grand geometrical gestures in front of the tables until the food has been eaten.

2. 'Magic Food': this is served from smallish bowls, covered on the outside with rough tactile materials. The bowl should be held in the left hand while the right is used to fish out the mysterious balls it contains: these will all be made of caramel, but each one filled with something different (such as candied fruits or bits of raw meat or garlic or mashed banana or chocolate or pepper) so that the diners cannot guess which flavour will enter the mouth next.

3. 'Tactile Vegetable Garden': A large plate containing a wide variety of raw and cooked green vegetables without any dressing or sauce is placed in front of each guest. The greens can be nibbled at will but only by burying the face in the plate, without the help of the hands, so as to inspire a true tasting with direct contact between the flavours and the textures of the green

leaves on the skin of the cheeks and the lips. Every time the diners raise their heads from the plate to chew, the waiters spray their faces with perfumes of lavender and eau de Cologne.

Between one dish and the next, since the dinner is completely based on tactile pleasures, the guests must let their fingertips feast uninterruptedly on their neighbour's pyjamas.

Formula by the Futurist Aeropainter
FILLÌA

Marinetti at the Winter Club Exhibition, Torino 1922. In the second row are Marinetti next to Francesco Cangiullo (left), Kanbara (far left) and the Japanese Futurist painter, Togo (right). In the front row are Diulgheroff (far left) and Fillìa.

synthesis of italy
dinner

Italy has always been in the past a gourmet food for foreigners. Today we too can taste her, though it is impossible if we want to savour all the flavours and perfumes of her orchards, meadows and gardens, to order on a single occasion all the various regional foods.

Therefore I suggest this meal which is a synthesis-of-Italy:

A square room with a blue ceiling, whose four walls are formed by enormous Futurist paintings on glass, representing: an alpine landscape by Depero — a landscape of lakes and plains with little hills in the background by Dottori — a volcanic landscape by Balla — a view of southern seas enlivened with little islands by Prampolini. Before eating the guests dye their hands blue with methylene.

At the beginning of the meal the first wall is illuminated from behind so that the white and brown mountains and the green pine trees rise up in geometric profile. In the room a temperature of spring freshness is maintained.

The first course is served: 'Alpine Dream': little ovoid lumps of ice wrapped in chestnut paste and laid on thick discs of sliced apple, dotted with nuts and bathed in Freisian wine.

The first wall darkens and the second is lit: the emeralds of the meadows and the reds of the farmhouses sparkle then lose themselves in the earth colours of the curving hills and the metallic blues of the lakes. The temperature in the room rises.

'Civilized rusticity': a cake of moulded boiled white rice on which are impressed large tender rose leaves, boned frog meat and very ripe cherries. While the guests eat the waiters quickly pass the warm scent of geraniums under their nostrils.

The second wall goes dark and the third is illuminated: the dynamic atmosphere of fiery Vesuvius. The climate in the room is summery.

'Suggestion of the South': a huge fennel bulb in which radishes and pitted olives are embedded. This is brought to the table wrapped in thin slices of roast lamb and immersed in wine from Capri.

The third wall darkens and the last is lit up: the splendour of the little islands shining in the bubbling foam of the sea. A sweltering temperature in the room.

'Colonial instinct': a colossal mullet stuffed with dates, bananas, orange slices, crabs, oysters and carobs is presented floating in a litre of Marsala. A violent perfume of carnations, broom and acacia is sprayed into the air.

At the end of the meal all four walls are lit and ices are served mixed with pineapple, raw pears and bilberries.

Formula by the Futurist Aeropainter
FILLÌA

geographic dinner

1. – A room in a restaurant decorated with aluminium and chromium tubing. The round windows disclose mysterious distant views of colonial landscapes.

2. – The diners, seated round a metal table its horizontal plane in linoleum, consult large atlases while invisible gramophones play loud Negro music.

3. – Once the meal has begun the *listavivande*-waitress enters the room, followed at a distance by the waiters: she is a shapely young woman dressed in a long white tunic on which a complete geographical map of Africa has been drawn in colour; it enfolds her entire body.

4. – The guests must choose the dish they want not according to its composition but by indicating on the geographical map the city or region that proves most seductive to their touristic imagination and spirit of adventure.

5. – Example: if a guest points his finger at the *listavivande*-waitress's left breast, where CAIRO is written, one of the waiters will silently disappear and return immediately with the dish that corresponds to that city. In this case: 'Love on the Nile', pyramids of stoned dates immersed in palm wine. Around the largest pyramid, juicy little cubes of cinnamon-flavoured mozzarella stuffed with roasted coffee beans and pistachios.

6. – If another diner points at the *listavivande*-waitress's right knee, the name ZANZIBAR, the waiter will serve him the 'Abibi Special': half a coconut, filled with chocolate and placed on a base of very finely chopped raw meat and steeped in Jamaican rum.

7. – And so it goes on, varying the geographical maps and the *listavivande*-waitresses for every dinner party and never letting anyone know the dishes in advance. In this way a gastronomic orientation inspired by continents, regions and cities, will prevail.

Formula by the Futurist Aeropainter
FILLÌA

new year's eve dinner

Nowadays habit has killed the joy in big dinners on New Year's Eve: for many years the same elements have conspired to produce a happiness which has been enjoyed too often. Everyone knows in advance the precise mechanism of events.

Family memories, felicitations and forecasts roll out like newspapers from presses. Old habits must be cast off to escape this monotony.

There are a thousand ways to revitalize this occasion: here is one which we put to the test with the Futursimultaneists in Rome: Mattia, Belli, D'Avila, Pandolfo, Battistella, Vignazia, etc.

At midnight after the endless chit-chat of waiting it is announced that dinner is served. In the dining room the tables have been removed and the guests are seated on chairs placed in a row, Indian file, one behind the other.

The inevitable turkey arrives, served by the waiters on metal plates: the turkey is stuffed with mandarins and salami.

Everyone eats in compulsory silence: the desire for noise and jollity is supressed.

Then suddenly a live turkey is let loose in the room, and it flounders about in terror, to the surprise of the men and the squeals of the women who can't understand this resurrection of the food they've just eaten. Order is re-established and everyone puts away his momentarily uncontained joy.

Beaten by the silence, in an attempt to start any sort of conversation one of those present says:

'I haven't yet expressed my good wishes for the New Year'.

Then as if following an order they all jump up and hurl themselves against the unwary conservator of tradition, whom they pummel repeatedly. Finally, happiness, exasperated by too much inaction, explodes and the guests disperse about the house, the most daring invading the kitchen.

The cook and two waiters are removed by force and everyone sets to thinking up a way of varying the meal. A fierce competition between the hot ovens, while frying pans and saucepans pass from hand to hand amidst laughter, shouts and a rain of ingredients.

Meanwhile others have discovered the wine cellar and thus an exceptional banquet is put together, which goes from kitchen to bedroom, from entrance hall to bathroom, to cellar. The dishes, put together almost by magic, follow one upon the other in the spirit of speed and harmony that animates the new cooks.

A guest tells the owner of the house:

'Fifteen years ago, on this same date ...'

But that same moment he is presented with a bowl full of spumante with cauliflowers, slices of lemon and roast beef floating in it: the memory of the past is shipwrecked in a stunning present.

The youngest guests shout:

'Bury your memories! We must start the year in a quite different way from the pre-war banquets!'

Three gramophones function as tables and from on top of the records, which have become rotating plates, people pluck little sugar-coated candies, cylinders of Parmesan cheese and hard-boiled eggs, while three different rhythms of Japanese music accompany the dynamic service.

The owner of the house suddenly turns out the lights. Stupefaction. In the darkness the voice of one of the guests is heard:

'This year we will succeed in breaking through the envelope of the atmosphere and reach the planets. I invite you all to a banquet next New Year's Eve on the moon, where we will finally taste foods of a flavour unknown to our palates and unimaginable drinks!'

Formula by the Futurist Aeropainter
FILLÌA

get-up-to-date dinner

Generally the difficulties of winning acceptance for a new way of eating are augmented by restaurant owners who, incapable or frightened, can't get it into their heads to renounce an antiquated way of cooking. All their worries are concentrated in helping their clients back into their coats.

If proprietors and employees would collaborate in their own interest to convince their clients of the necessity of a more modern way of eating, most doubts and disbeliefs could be overcome and restaurants would no longer be grey places of unvarying habits.

To regular clients when they come in and ask for their usual plate of spaghetti the waiter ought to give this short, clarifying speech:

'From today our kitchen has banished pastasciutta. We have come to this decision because pasta is made of long silent archeological worms which, like their brothers living in the dungeons of history, weigh down the stomach make it ill render it useless. You musn't introduce these white worms into the body unless you want to make it as closed dark and immobile as a museum.'

The Italian of our high speed era cannot but heed such an argument. The waiter will then serve him this 'Get Up To Date' dinner: rice, boiled then fried in butter, compressed inside little balls of raw lettuce, sprinkled with grappa and served on a *poltiglia* of fresh tomatoes and boiled potatoes.

Formula by the Futurist Aeropainter
FILLÌA

improvized dinner

These improvized dinners are recommended as a means of bringing together maximum originality, variety, surprise, unexpectedness and good humour.

Of every cook it is asked that he acquire an attitude that:

– understands that form and colour are just as important as taste.

– can conceive of an original architecture for every dish, possibly different for each individual, in such a way that EVERY PERSON HAS THE SENSATION OF EATING not just good food but also WORKS OF ART.

– will, before preparing a dinner, study the character and sensibility of everyone, and take account *of age, sex, physical make-up and even psychological factors* in the distribution of the dishes.

– can when necessary create dinners in motion, by means of moving carpets that run along in front of the diners, carrying every kind of different dish: individualized preparation would be simplified this way because everyone would be thrust into a position where he would have to seize his preferred food for himself. And the choosing would be doubly agreeable because in a certain sense it would encourage the human spirit of adventure and heroism.

At improvized dinners the cooks, waiters and managers can of course discuss the attributes of the various dishes, but they must *never* take into account the personal taste of the diners.

Formula·by the Futurist Aeropainter
FILLÌA

declaration of love
dinner

A shy lover yearns to express his feelings to a beautiful and intelligent woman. The following Declaration of Love Dinner served on the terrace of a grand hotel in the twinkling night of the city will help him to achieve this aim.

I Desire You: antipasto composed of a myriad selection of exquisite tid-bits, which the waiter will only let them admire, while She contents herself with bread and butter.

Flesh Adored: A big plate made from a shining mirror. In the centre, chicken slices perfumed with amber and covered with a thin layer of cherry jam. She, while eating, will admire her reflection in the plate.

This Is How I'll Love You: Little tubes of pastry filled with many different flavours, one of plums, one of apples cooked in rum, one of potatoes drenched in cognac, one of sweet rice, etc. She, without batting an eyelid, will eat them all.

Super Passion: A very compact cake of sweet pastry with small cavities on the top filled with anise, glacier mints, rum, juniper and Amaro.

Tonight With Me: A very ripe orange enclosed in a large hollowed-out sweet pepper, embedded in a thick zabaglione flavoured with juniper and salted with little bits of oyster and drops of sea water.

Formula by the Futurist Aeropainter
FILLÌA

holy supper

To the Futurist clerics who have been visiting the apartment of the engineeer Barosi and Dr Vernazza in Turin, which contains Futurist religious paintings, a dinner of the following composition is offered:

Lined up on a big table are twenty glasses all the same size but containing in different proportions: mineral water coloured red — white wine from the Castelli Romani coloured blue with methylene — cold milk coloured orange.

In front of the glasses, laid out on twenty aluminum plates are: slices of assorted meats masked by a pineapple *poltiglia* — raw onions covered in jam — fish fillets buried in whipped cream and zabaglione — buttered rolls spread with caviare inside a large pumpkin.

The clerics must choose without hesitation, by listening with compunction to any divine inspiration which may come their way.

Formula by the Futurist Aeropainter
FILLÌA

a simultaneous dinner

For businessmen unable in the whirl of affairs to get to a restaurant or return home a simultaneous meal will be designed which will allow them to continue various activities (writing walking talking) and eat contemporaneously:

A big smoker's pipe of lacquered red metal with a little electric oven will cook a soup.

Some small 'thermos' bottles in the form of fountain pens, filled with hot chocolate.

Some pocket diaries will contain fish pastilles.

Letters and invoices of different strengths of perfume will be available in a file to calm, satisfy or excite the appetite.

Formula by the Futurist Aeropainter
FILLÌA

dinner
of white desire

Ten Negroes, each holding a lily in his hand, gather round a table in a city by the sea, overwhelmed by an indefinable emotion that makes them long to conquer the countries of Europe with a mixture of spiritual yearning and erotic desire.

The whole room is sunk in mysterious half-light and the invisible lamps allow only sufficient brightness to see the table, covered by a layer of dark shining glass.

Without a word a Negro woman cook serves them twenty fresh white eggs which have been punctured at both ends to inject the insides with a delicate perfume of acacia flowers: the Negroes inhale the contents of the eggs, without breaking the shells.

Then a large tureen is brought full of cold milk in which are floating little cubes of mozzarella cheese and sweet white Muscat grapes.

The Negroes' state of mind is affected as it were unconsciously by the paleness and whiteness of all the foods.

The Negro cook returns again with a tray laden with pieces of coconut studded with nougat, enclosed in layers of butter and arranged on a bed of boiled rice and whipped cream. Contemporaneously they drink undiluted anise, grappa or gin.

The sensibilities of the Negroes feed on the white flavour colour odour of the food, while from the ceiling an incandescent globe of milky glass descends towards the table and a smell of jasmine fills the room.

Formula by the Futurist Aeropainter
FILLÌA

astronomical dinner

The table is made of a sheet of crystal placed on shining aluminium legs. The dining room is completely dark. Sources of variable light on the underside of the table, moving through the layer of crystal from bottom to top, and in from the two sides towards the centre, illuminate the crystal surface in a hundred different ways, the intensity and colour varying with the foods.

All the plates, bowls and cups are made of crystal.

Dawn will thus rise within the crystal goblets in the form of a perfect *consumato* made fluorescent with a tiny quantity of 'fluorescin'.

High noon will be a mosaic of smoked meat, pistachios and red pepper, sprinkled with lemon and delicately perfumed with vanilla will rise in the sky.

Sunset will consist of a dish of very thin slices of smoked salmon, beetroot and oranges.

Then, in the deep night of the room, a cosmographic sphere of ice-cream (50 centimetres in diameter), the only illuminated body, will move very slowly across the crystal surface which now seems to hang suspended in the darkness.

A pump in the shape of a telescope will launch parabolas of Asti spumante.

Formula by the Futurist
Dr. SIROCOFRAN

One of a set of dishes for a 'Life of Marinetti' cycle designed by Giuseppe Mazzotti, 1939.

Marinetti, Sudan-Parigi Tactile Painting (1920), private collection.

Marinetti with the poet Tullio d'Albisola.

(More than 80 recipes for Futurist dishes have been described already in detail in the chapter 'Provocative Dinners'.)

futurist formulas for restaurants and quisibeve

(The vague quantities given in many of these formulas, far from constituting a matter of concern, should on the contrary stimulate the imagination of Futurist cooks, for fortuitous mistakes often lead to new dishes.)

Decisone
(polibibita by the Futurist Aeropoet Marinetti)

> 1/4 China Martini
> 1/4 rum
> 1/4 boiling Barolo
> 1/4 mandarin juice

Inventina
((polibibita by the Futurist Aeropoet Marinetti)

> 1/3 Asti spumante
> 1/3 pineapple liqueur
> 1/3 chilled orange juice

A Simultaneous Dish
(formula by the Futurist Aeropoet Marinetti)

Chicken aspic, half of it studded with squares of raw young camel meat rubbed with garlic and smoked, and half studded with balls of hare meat stewed in wine.
Eat this by washing down every mouthful of camel with a sip of acqua del Serino and every mouthful of hare with a sip of Scirà (a non-alcoholic Turkish wine made with must).

Words In Liberty Sea Platter
(formula by the Futurist Aeropoet Marinetti)

On a sea of endive dotted with bits of ricotta sails half a watermelon with a tiny captain on board, sculpted out of Dutch cheese, who commands a sluggish crew roughly hewn in calves' brains cooked in milk. A few centimetres from the prow a rocky reef of Sienese Panforte. The sea and the ship are sprinkled with cinnamon or red pepper.

Traidue

(formula by the Futurist Aeropainter Fillìa)

Two rectangular pieces of bread: one spread with anchovy paste, the other with chopped apple skins. Between the two slices of bread salami.

Totalrice

(formula by the Futurist Aeropainter Fillìa)

Boiled white rice is arranged like this: one part in the middle of the plate in the form of a hemisphere, another part around the hemisphere in the form of a crown. The moment it is brought to the table pour over the hemisphere a sauce of hot white wine thickened with cornflour and over the crown a sauce of hot beer, egg yolk and Parmesan cheese.

Italian Sea

(formula by the Futurist Aeropainter Fillìa)

On a rectangular plate arrange a base formed of geometric stripes of fresh tomato sauce and liquidized spinach to create a precise red and green pattern. On this green and red sea place some little constructions made of tiny cutlets of boiled fish, banana slices, a cherry and a piece of dried fig. Each of these constructions is rendered organic by a toothpick holding the various elements together vertically.

Sculpted Meat

(formula by the Futurist Aeropainter Fillìa)

'Sculpted Meat' (a synthetic interpretation of the orchards, gardens and pastures of Italy) is composed of a large cylindrical rissole of minced veal stuffed with eleven different kinds of cooked vegetables. This cylinder (A), standing upright in the middle of the plate, is crowned with a thick layer of honey (C) and supported at the bottom by a sausage ring (B) which rests on three golden spheres of chicken meat (D).

Aerofood
(formula by the Futurist Aeropainter Fillìa)

The diner is served from the right with a plate containing some black olives, fennel hearts and kumquats. From the left he is served with a rectangle made of sandpaper, silk and velvet. The foods must be carried directly to the mouth with the right hand while the left hand lightly and repeatedly strokes the tactile rectangle. In the meantime the waiters spray the napes of the diners' necks with a *conprofumo* of carnations while from the kitchen comes contemporaneously a violent *conrumore* of an aeroplane motor and some *dismusica* by Bach.

The Excited Pig
(formula by the Futurist Aeropainter Fillìa)

A whole salami, skinned, is served upright on a dish containing some very hot black coffee mixed with a good deal of eau de Cologne.

Edible Alphabet
(formula by the Futurist Aeropainter Fillìa)

From some Bolognese mortadella sausage, cheese, pastry and caramel cut out the letters of the alphabet (thick enough for them to be able to stand upright): each diner gets two, to match the initials of his name; this then resolves which foods are eaten with which.

Sicilian Headland
(formula by the Futurist Aeropainter Fillìa)

Chop together tuna, apples, olives and little Japanese nuts. Spread the resulting paste on a cold egg and jam omelette.

Immortal Trout

(formula by the Futurist Aeropainter Fillìa)

Stuff some trout with chopped nuts and fry them in olive oil. Then wrap the trout in very thin slices of calves' liver.

Hunting in Heaven

(formula by the Futurist Aeropainter Fillìa)

Slowly cook a hare in sparkling wine mixed with cocoa powder until the liquid is absorbed. Then immerse it for a minute in plenty of lemon juice. Serve it in a copious green sauce based on spinach and juniper, and decorate with those silver hundreds and thousands which recall huntsmen's shot.

Devil in Black Key

(polibibita by the Aeropainter Fillìa)

    2/4 orange juice

    1/4 grappa

    1/4 liquid chocolate

Put in a hard-boiled egg yolk.

Elasticake

(formula by the Futurist Aeropainter Fillìa)

Fill a ball of puff pastry with some red zabaglione and insert a stick (3 cm) of liquorice. Close the top part of the ball with half a prune.

The Great Waters
(polibibita by the Futurist Aeropainter Prampolini)

> 1/4 grappa
> 1/4 gin
> 1/4 kummel
> 1/4 anise liqueur

On the liquid float a square of anchovy paste wrapped pharmaceutically in a wafer.

Alcoholic Joust
(polibibita by the Futurist Aeropainter Prampolini)

> 2/4 dry red Barbera wine
> 1/4 citronade
> 1/4 Campari bitters

Into the liquid put a square of cheese and a square of chocolate threaded on a toothpick.

Tasty Preface
(formula by the Futurist Aeropainter Prampolini)

A cylinder of butter with a green olive on top. At the base of the cylinder: salami, raisins, pine nuts and tiny sugared sweets.

Equator + North Pole
(formula by the Futurist Aeropainter Prampolini)

An equatorial sea of golden poached egg yolks, served like oysters with pepper, salt and lemon. In the centre a cone of stiffly-whipped and solidified egg white rises dotted with orange segments like succulent pieces of the sun. The peak of the cone is bombarded by bits of black truffle shaped to look like black aeroplanes trying to conquer the zenith.

Tasty Discs
(formula by the Futurist Aeropainter Prampolini)

A tart of various fruits which rests on a disc of chocolate. The tart is then covered with two layers of *poltiglia* which divide it in half: the first made of tomato sauce and the second of spinach.

Spring Paradox
(formula by the Futurist Aeropainter Prampolini)

A big cylinder of plain ice cream has peeled bananas standing on top of it to look like palm trees. Hide some hard-boiled eggs, with their yolks removed and filled with plum jam, among the bananas.

Rice Herodias
(formula by the Futurist Dr. Sirocofran)

To glorify the highest virginal purity and at the same time unite it with the greatest voluptuousness in the way of perfume, and to honour thus the glorious name of Mallarmé, who poetized the virgin Herodias in a green and watery landscape scattered with deeply sensual purple irises, take some rice and cook it in plenty of milk salted to taste. Drain it and sprinkle with finely-powdered orris root.

Captive Perfumes
(formula by the Futurist Dr. Sirocofran)

Put a drop of perfume inside some thin brightly- coloured balloons. Blow them up and warm them gently to vaporize the perfume and swell the outer surface.
Bring them to the table contemporaneously with the coffee, in little warmed dishes, making sure the perfumes are various. Hold a lighted cigarette near the bladders and inhale the scents the escapes.

Dates in Moonlight
(formula by the Futurist Dr. Sirocofran)

35-40 very mature and sugary dates, 500 grams Roman ricotta. Stone the dates and mash them well (all the better if you can pass them through a sieve). Mix the pulp thus obtained with the ricotta until you have a smooth *poltiglia*. Refrigerate for a few hours and serve chilled.

Folgore's Dazzling Appetizer
(formula by the Futurist poet Luciano Folgore)

Awake my friend, for if you sleep
you will not make this superb dish —
an antipasto from blue sea deep —
for he who sleeps will catch no fish
but catch you must if you wish to dine
so fish for your fish in a barrel of brine
for two fine herring smooth as silk,
and bathe them in a little milk.
Now pick them up these slippery fish
and clean them well, inside and out,
leave the milk in a small round dish
(you'll need it later on no doubt).
But oh! these herrings from out of the oak
are still so salty — they must soak
at least four hours in acqua pura
to de-salt them you'll never be surer
Don't moon about but lay them out
with a little onion and a hard-boiled egg
and chop them fine with a half-moon shine
(or a cutting knife I hear you beg!),
chop on and on but make no haste
till what is left is an antipasto paste
to which add condiments to taste.

This done, take the milk in the little round bowl
add a few drops of vinegar and some oil
mix all together as much as you want
for a sauce that's bland yet saucily piquant,
and over the herrings you've finished chopping
this makes a most delicious topping.
An antipasto such as this is
will start a meal that ends in kisses
rousing every appetite!
It's said that a King of Patagonia
for such a food renounced his nation
and while untrue — o mama mia!
There's no better recommendation.
This dish that I command to you —
so good to the appetite and true —
It seems that Dante in the *Vita Nuova*
did write of it when the Banquet was over.
"Dear friend — such joy! you cannot buy it!
Nor can you judge if you don't try it."

Futurist Risotto with Cape Gooseberries

(formula by the Futurist Aeropoet Paolo Buzzi)

To prepare, remove the thin outside sheath from a kilo of Cape gooseberries and chop them into small pieces, carefully reserving any juice
which escapes.
Get ready separately a large quantity of sauce made with a big bunch
of parsley pounded together with a hint of garlic and onion.
Put lots of oil in a saucepan.
When it's hot take it from the heat and add the chopped gooseberries
(reserving the juice) and the parsley sauce.
Return to the heat: cook until everything begins to take colour (but the
onion not brown) then add enough rice for six persons, stirring cons-
tantly until it becomes golden. At this point ladle by ladle add seasoned
stock to which the gooseberry juice has been added.

After twenty minutes of cooking, remove from the fire, forking up the rice and adding lots of cheese.

This risotto is Futurist because the Cape gooseberry is a fruit as it were *outside our normal frame of reference*: certainly much more so than the saffron plant which − nevertheless − is scarcely to be found growing wild any more either.

It is *synthetic* because the eight grains enclosed in the sour bulb of the fruit are like the 'Marinettians' eight souls in a bomb; and because the Cape gooseberry is winged with wings of strong material like an aeroplane, wings that one throws away; and then they resemble parachutes; and it is extremely quickly digested like everything that comes from the Futurist forge (I mean kitchen).

Rice Oranges

(formula by the Futurist Word-In-Liberty poet Mazza)

Prepare a good saffron or tomato risotto, being careful to take it from the fire not *al dente* but well-cooked, and let it cool. (It must not be *al dente* because the grains of rice should stick to each other).

Wet your hands, or, even better, oil them with olive oil, and make little balls out of it about the size of an orange. With your finger make a hole in each, enlarge it without breaking the walls, and fill it with some roughly-chopped braised meat and some of the juices in which it was cooked. Add little lumps of cheese (fontina, mozzarella, caciocavallo or fresh provalone), salami or prosciutto crudo in little pieces, pine nuts and raisins. Cover with more risotto and form into a ball again. Roll these oranges in white flour then in beaten egg and finally in breadcrumbs. Fry them in lots of olive oil until golden and serve them hot and crisp.

Like A Cloud
(formula by the Futurist Aeropoet Giulio Onesti)

A great mound of whipped cream streaked with orange juice, mint, strawberry jam and sprinkled lightly with Asti spumante.

Steel Chicken
(formula by the Futurist Aeropainter Diulgheroff)

Roast a chicken, emptied of its insides. As soon as it is cold, make an opening in the back and fill the inside with red zabaglione on which are laid two hundred grams of silver hundreds and thousands. Attach cockscombs all round the opening.

Words-In-Liberty
(formula by the Futurist Aeropoet Escadamè)

Three sea dates, a half-moon of red watermelon, a thicket of radicchio, a little cube of Parmesan, a little sphere of gorgonzola, 8 tiny balls of caviare, 2 figs, 5 amaretti di Saronno biscuits: all arranged neatly on a large bed of mozzarella, to be eaten, eyes closed, letting one's hands wander here and there, while the great painter and word-in-liberty poet Depero recites his famous song 'Jacopson'.

The Gulf of Trieste
(formula by the Futurist Aeropoet Bruno Sanzin)

Cook a kilo of shelled mussels in an onion and garlic sauce, slowly adding the rice. Serve this risotto with a dish of unsugared vanilla cream.

The Drunken Calf

(formula by the Futurist Aeropoet Bruno Sanzin)

Fill some uncooked veal with chopped apples, nuts, pine nuts and cloves. Cook in the oven. Serve cold in a bath of Asti spumante or Passito wine from Lipari.

Simultaneous Ice-Cream

(Formula by the Futurist word-in-liberty poet Giuseppe Steiner)

Dairy cream and little squares of raw onion frozen together.

Ultravirile

(formula by the Futurist art critic P.A. Saladin)

On a rectangular plate put some thin slices of calf's tongue, boiled and cut lengthwise. On top of these arrange lengthwise along the axis of the plate two parallel rows of spit-roasted prawns. Between these two rows place the body of a lobster, previously boned and shelled, covered in green zabaglione. At the tail end of the lobster place three halves of hard-boiled egg, cut lengthwise, so that the yellow rests on the slices of tongue. The front part, however, is crowned with six cockscombs laid out like sectors of a circle, while completing the garnish are two rows of little cylinders composed of a little wheel of lemon, slices of grape and a slice of truffle sprinkled with lobster coral.

Carnaleap
(polibibita by the Futurist art critic P.A. Saladin)

3 coffee beans.
1 part liqueur made from the following plants: coca, cola,
damiana, muira puama, yohimbin, gingseng and prickly pear.
1 part tea liqueur.
1 part Kirsch.

More-Less-By-Division
(polibibita by the Futurist art critic P.A. Saladin)

1 candied chestnut.
1 part rose liqueur.
1 part pineapple liqueur.
1 part liqueur of thyme or serpolet.

Alpine Love
(polibibita by the Futurist art critic P.A. Saladin)

1/4 lemon balm liqueur.
1/4 spruce liqueur.
1/4 banana liqueur.
1/4 lily of the valley liqueur.

Fog Lifter
(polibibita by the Futurist art critic P.A. Saladin)

1/3 wormwood liqueur.
1/3 rhubarb liqueur.
1/3 grappa.

A Spark

(polibibita by the Futurist art critic P.A. Saladin)

        1/4 green walnut liqueur
        1/4 gentian liqueur
        1/4 absinthe liqueur
        1/4 juniper liqueur

Manandwomanatmidnight

(formula by the Futurist art critic P.A. Saladin)

Pour some red zabaglione onto a round plate so as to form a large pool.

In the middle of this place a nice big onion ring transfixed by a stalk of candied angelica. Then lay out two candied chestnuts, as shown in the illustration, and serve one plate per couple.

Fisticuff Stuff

(formula by the Futurist art critic P.A. Saladin)

Cover the bottom of a round plate with fondue lightly perfumed with grappa. On one side of the plate put equidistant from each other three halves of red pepper shaped into cones which have been cooked in the oven and filled with a green paste composed of asparagus tips, celery and fennel hearts, little onions, capers, artichokes and olives. On the opposite side set out in a row three boiled leeks. An arabesque of grated truffle which starts at the second pepper and winds its way finally to the one on the edge completes the dish.

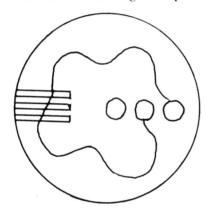

Cubist Vegetable Patch

(formula by the Futurist art critic P.A. Saladin)

1. Little cubes of celery from Verona fried and sprinkled with paprika;
2. Little cubes of fried carrot sprinkled with grated horseradish;

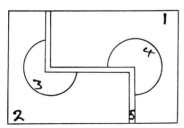

3. Boiled peas;
4. Little pickled onions from Ivrea sprinkled with chopped parsley;
5. Little bars of Fontina cheese;

N.B. The cubes must not be larger than 1 cubic centimetre.

White and Black

(formula by the Futurist Poet of National Record Farfa)

A one-man-show on the internal walls of the Stomach consisting of free-form arabesques of whipped cream sprinkled with lime-tree charcoal. Contra the blackest indigestion. Pro the whitest teeth.

The Soil of Pozzuoli
and the Greenery of Verona

(formula by the Futurist Poet of National Record Farfa)

Candied citrons, stuffed with chopped fried cuttlefish. Chew them up well as if they were anti-Futurist critics.

Strawberry Breasts

(formula by the Futurist Poet of National Record Farfa)

A pink plate with two erect feminine breasts made of ricotta dyed pink with Campari with nipples of candied strawberry. More fresh strawberries under the covering of ricotta making it possible to bite into an ideal multiplication of imaginary breasts.

Geraniums on a Spit
(formula by the Futurist Poet of National Record Farfa)

Long slender cylinders of puff pastry. Thread onto each one four geraniums: white, pink, red, and purple, having first lightly browned them in cold rosolio liqueur or in Roob Coccola di Zara. While eating them think of the dead floral style.

Carrot + Trousers = Professor
(formula by the Futurist Poet of National Record Farfa)

A raw carrot standing upright, with the thin part at the bottom, where two boiled aubergines are attached with a toothpick to look like violet trousers in the act of marching. Leave the green leaves on the top of the carrot to represent the hope of a pension. Eat the whole thing without ceremony!

Manna Coffee
(formula by the Futurist Poet of National Record Farfa)

Barley coffee roasted and sweetened with manna. Serve it very hot so that the diners can cool it by blowing over it densely congealing jokes.

Senate of the Digestion
(formula by the Futurist Poet of National Record Farfa)

Four diners will each order two well-known dishes or digestive drinks. Or eight diners one each. The other guests will secretly vote against one or the other. The winner will be the drink or dish that gets the fewest negative votes.

Libyan Aeroplane

(formula by the air pilot, Futurist poet and Aeropainter Fedele Azari)

Steep candied chestnuts for 2 minutes in eau de Cologne and then for
3 minutes in milk, then serve them on a *poltiglia* (shaped into the form
of a slender aeroplane) of bananas, apples, dates and peas.

Network in the Sky

(formula by the Futurist Aerosculptor Mino Rosso)

The base is a disc of cherry-flavoured caramel.
The large cylinder: three leaves of puff pastry stuffed with tamarind pulp
and covered with chocolate fondant.
The small cylinder: crowns of meringue one on top of the other covered
in mandarin-flavoured fondant.
The centre of the upper cylinder contains whipped cream with tamarind
pulp and shelled pistachios.

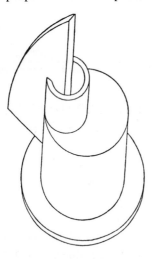

The wing is mandarin-flavoured caramel.
Shortly before bringing it to the table the pudding should be covered
with threads of green spun sugar.

Intuitive Antipasto
(formula by Signora Colombo-Fillìa)

Hollow out an orange to form a little basket in which are placed different kinds of salami, some butter, some pickled mushrooms, anchovies and green peppers. The basket perfumes the various elements with orange. Inside the peppers are hidden little cards printed with a Futurist phrase or a surprising saying (for example: 'Futurism is an anti-historical movement' – 'Live dangerously' – 'With Futurist cooking, doctors, pharmacists and grave diggers will be out of work,' etc.)

Milk in a Green Light
(formula by Signorina Germana Colombo)

Put a few teaspoons of honey, lots of black grapes and several red radishes in a large bowl of cold milk. Eat with a green *disluce* illuminating the bowl. Contemporaneously drink a *polibibita* made up of mineral water, beer and blackberry juice.

Futurist Pheasant
(formula by the Aeropoet Dr Pino Masnata)

Roast a well-cleaned pheasant, then keep it for an hour in a *bain-marie* in Muscat wine from Syracuse. Then an hour in milk. Fill it with mostarda di Cremona** and candied fruits.

Piquant Airport
(formula by the Futurist Aeropainter Caviglioni)

A field of Russian salad with mayonnaise, covered with green salad. All around various medallions composed of rolls spread with orange, egg white and mixed fruit. With red-coloured butter and anchovies or sardines form the outlines of aeroplanes on the green field.

Roars of Ascent
(Rice with Oranges)
(formula by the Futurist Aeropainter Caviglioni)

Plain risotto with a luminous sauce: the sauce is composed of the marrow from a veal bone braised in Marsala and a little rum and orange peel cut into thin strips, boiled with a hint of vinegar. And orange juice. Perfume with 'national sauce', which you can find in the shops.

Veal Fuselage
(formula by the Futurist Aeropainter Caviglioni)

Slices of veal attached to a fuselage composed of cooked chestnuts, little onions and sausages. All sprinkled with powdered chocolate.

Cosmic Apparitions
(formula by the Futurist Aeropainter Caviglioni)

Fennel, beetroot, turnips, yellow carrots on top of a spinach pie. Add some candy floss. The boiled and buttered vegetables are cut in the form of stars, moons, etc.

Digestive Landing
(formula by the Futurist Aeropainter Caviglioni)

Out of a sweet *poltiglia* of chestnuts boiled in water and vanilla sticks form a landscape of mountains and plains.
Above it, with blue ice cream, form atmospheric layers and streak them with aeroplanes of pastry coming down at an angle towards the ground.

Italian Breasts in the Sunshine
(formula by the Futurist Aeropainter Marisa Mori)

Form two firm half spheres of almond paste. Place a fresh strawberry on the centre of each of them. Then pour some zabaglione onto the plate and some dollops of whipped cream.
The whole may be sprinkled with strong pepper and garnished with sweet red peppers.

Tyrrhenian Seaweed Foam (with coral garnish)
(formula by the Futurist aeroceramist Tullio d'Albasola)

Take a bunch of freshly-netted sea lettuce, being careful the catch was not made near sewers or drains because such lettuce easily absorbs bad smells. Wash and rinse in plenty of running water. When it is clean, dip it in some lemon juice. Powder the leaves with sugar and add spray with a wave of whipped cream.
The coral garnish consists of an assembly of clusters of piquant red peppers, slices of sea urchins caught at full moon, and a constellation of seeds from a ripe pomegranate.
The whole, with its artistic architectural lines and inspired arabesques, should be served immediately on a round flat plate, with waves made of broth added, and covered by a sheet of blue cellophane.

Marinettian Bombe
(formula by the Futurist cook Alicata)

Coat a bombe mould with orange gelatine, decorating the top with little strawberries. Decorate the sides with some candied angelica in the form of a crown and the back part with candied chestnuts. Cover the decoration with another layer of gelatine and leave it to set.
Line the empty centre with some sponge fingers, forming a square and fill up the space with a vanilla bavaroise. Chill it thoroughly, then unmould it and serve with a garnish of half apricots in gelatine, orange slices and bits of candied lemon.

The Tummy Tickler
(formula by the Futurist Aeropainter Ciuffo)

A slice of pineapple on which sardines are laid out in rays. The centre of the pineapple slice is covered with a layer of tuna on which sits half a nut.

Sweet and Strong
(formula by Signora Barosi)

A *traidue* of two slices of bread and butter, spread with mustard and enclosing bananas and anchovies.

Fire In The Mouth
(polibibita by the Futurist engineer Barosi)

At the bottom of a glass: whisky with liqueur cherries, previously rolled in cayenne pepper. Next layer: milk and honey or honey (1 cm thick) forming an impermeable division. On top of the honey: alkermes, vermouth and Strega.

An Upright
(polibibita by the Futurist engineer Barosi)

A small empty cylinder of ice, covered outside with honey. Inside and at the base: dairy ice cream, then nuts from Chivasso and pieces of pineapple, the whole thing steeped in vermouth and crushed glacier mints.

Before the Wedding Ring
(polibibita by the Futurist engineer Barosi)

On an aluminum pan, equidistant: a little heap of toasted almonds, banana slices, anchovies, roasted coffee beans, tomato slices, slices of Parmesan cheese. In the centre of the pan, a glass containing vermouth, cognac, Strega. Inside: banana slices.

The Regenerator
(formula by the Futurist engineer Barosi)

an egg yolk.
half a glass of Asti spumante.
3 toasted nuts.
3 teaspoons of sugar.
Beat the whole together for ten minutes. Serve in a glass with a peeled banana sticking out of it.

The Lictor's Bundle
(formula by the Futurist engineer Barosi)

Cardoon and celery sticks, about 10 cm long, cooked previously in water, are placed upright so as to form an empty cylinder. They are fixed by: underneath a hemisphere of plain risotto and above by half a lemon. The inside of the cylinder is filled with chopped meat, oil, pepper and salt. Distributed like stars on the hemisphere of rice: a cucumber, a piece of banana, a piece of beetroot.

Simultaneity

(polibibita by the Futurist Dr Vernazza)

4/8 Vernaccia wine.
3/8 vermouth.
1/8 aquavit.

Some very fresh dates, stuffed with mascarpone cheese mixed with Aurum liqueur (Pescara). Thus prepared the dates are then wrapped in thin slices of prosciutto crudo and then in a lettuce leaf. The whole thing is threaded on a toothpick along with a little pickled red pepper stuffed with bits of Parmesan cheese.

(If the toothpick is put into the glass, eyes of fat deposited by the ham will appear on the surface of the liquid: in this case the *polibibita* may be called 'This little piggy who makes eyes at you').

Risotto Trinacria

(Formula by the Futurist Dr Vernazza)

Rice cooked in the normal way. Sauce prepared by frying a little onion and butter, to which you add a tiny bit of flaked white tuna and tomato. Season the risotto, mix in a few green olives and garnish with well-peeled mandarin segments.

Tennis Chop
(formula by the Futurist Dr. Vernazza)

Veal cutlets cooked in butter and cut in the form of tennis rackets. Before serving, spread them with a thick layer of a paste (made of mascarpone and chopped nuts); trace lines on the paste with tomato sauce mixed with rum. To make the racket handle, an anchovy with a slice of banana on top.

Then some perfectly round balls made from cherries soaked in liqueur (without stones), rolled in a paste of ricotta, egg, cheese and nutmeg. Cook rapidly to prevent the alcohol from losing strength.

Black Shirt Snack
(formula by the Futurist Dr. Vernazza)

A fish cutlet between two large discs of rennet apple: the whole doused in rum and set alight before serving.

Atlantic Aerofood
(formula by the Futurist Dr. Vernazza)

Bright green vegetable *poltiglia* (made of lentils, peas, spinach, etc.). On this place some aeroplanes, one per diner, formed by: little triangular pastries (wings) – carrots cut lengthwise (fuselage) – cockscombs cooked in butter (rudder) – kumquats cut in round slices and set upright (propeller).

Edible Skier

(formula by the Futurist Dr. Vernazza)

Zabaglione frozen hard in a bowl. On top: a layer of whipped cream.
Between the zabaglione and the cream slices of orange soaked in Zara
maraschino.

On the white surface place long slices of banana with, at the centre,
a half date stuffed with a paste of chopped sweet and bitter almonds
and Aurum liqueur. On the two sides of this composition, which reminds
one of skis: discs of candied fruits with a sweet breadstick threaded
through the centre.

Diabolical Roses

(formula by the Futurist Pasca d'Angelo)

> 2 eggs.
> 100 gr. flour.
> juice of 1/2 fresh lemon.
> a tablespoon of olive oil.

Mix the ingredients well to form a not too thick batter; pluck the heads
off some velvety red roses in full bloom, toss them in, and fry them in
boiling oil the same way as with Jerusalem artichokes. Serve very hot.
(These roses are ideal for newly weds to eat at midnight in January especially if they are covered with Mafarka pudding. — See the following
formula).

Mafarka Pudding

(formula by the Futurist Pasca d'Angelo)

> 50 gr. coffee.
> sugar to taste.
> 100 gr. rice.

166

2 eggs.
rind of fresh lemon.
50 gr. orange flower water.
1/2 litre milk.

Cook the coffee in the milk and sweeten to taste. Pour in the rice and cook it until very dry and al dente. Remove from the heat and when it is cold grate into it the peel of a lemon and stir in the orange flower water; pour into a mould and refrigerate. When icy cold serve with fresh biscuits.
Buon appetito, and long live steel!

The Bombardment of Adrianopolis

(formula by the Futurist Pasca d'Angelo)

2 eggs.
100 gr. olives.
50 gr. capers.
100 gr. buffalo mozzarella.
6 anchovies.
25 gr. butter.
100 gr. rice.
1/2 litre milk.

Set the rice to cook in the milk and half way through the cooking add the butter and some salt. Remove the rice from the heat and quickly mix in an egg, incorporating it well. When the mixture is cold divide it into ten parts, and into each incorporate a slice of mozzarella, half an anchovy, three or four capers, two or three stoned olives and a good pinch of black pepper. Beat the other egg, form each portion into a ball, dip it in the egg, then roll in breadcrumbs and fry.

The Jumping Askari (An East African soldier)
(formula by the Futurist Giachino, proprietor of the Holy Palate)

Cook a leg of lamb with bay leaves, pepper, rosemary and garlic. Strain off the juices and serve with dates stuffed with salted pistachios, some dry white wine and lemon juice.

Appetite Appeaser
(formula by the Futurist Giachino, proprietor of the Holy Palate)

On a large slice of ham put raw salami, gherkins, olives, tuna, pickled mushrooms, artichoke hearts. Bring the two ends of the ham together and seal them with anchovy fillets, a slice of pineapple and some butter.

Zoological Soup
(formula by the Futurist Giachino, proprietor of the Holy Palate)

Pastry in animal shapes, made of rice flour and eggs, filled with jam and served in a hot pink broth spiked with a few drops of Italian eau de Cologne.

Compenetration
(formula by the Futurist Giachino, proprietor of the Holy Palate)

On top of some creamed peas place a cutlet of smoked meat cooked in butter. Pour some tomato sauce on to the cutlet and add an apple with anchovies soaked in egg and rum. Dip the stuffed turnips in egg yolk and then in fine breadcrumbs and cook them in the oven.

Green Rice

(formula by the Futurist Giachino, proprietor of the Holy Palate)

On a base of spinach pour some white boiled rice with butter. Cover this with a thick cream of peas and ground pistachios.

Divorced Eggs

(formula by the Futurist Giachino, proprietor of the Holy Palate)

Divide some hard-boiled eggs in half and remove the yolks intact. Put the yolks on a *poltiglia* of potatoes and the whites on a *poltiglia* of carrots.

Pocket Book Turnips

(formula by the Futurist Giachino, proprietor of the Holy Palate)

Small new turnips boiled for 10 minutes with bay leaves, onions and rosemary. Slice them open like a wallet and stuff them with anchovies soaked in egg and rum. Dip the stuffed turnips in egg yolk and then in fine breadcrumbs and cook them in the oven.

Mouth of Fire

(formula by the Futurist Giachino, proprietor of the Holy Palate)

Brown some marrow from a shin of veal in butter. Then add some breadcrumbs, nuts and a juniper berry and put it back on the heat with half a glass of plum juice and cook it until all the liquid has been absorbed. Then add six stoned plums stuffed with almonds. Return to the heat with a cup of dry white wine and lemon juice.

White Rose

(polibibita by the Futurist Giachino, proprietor of the Holy Palate)

Various quantities of orangeade, Campari and anise with essence of White Roses.

Surprise Bananas

(formula by the Futurist Piccinelli, cook at the Holy Palate)

Scoop out a cavity in a peeled banana and fill it with chopped chicken meat.
Put it on the fire in a buttered pan and gradually add some meat juices. Serve with vegetables.

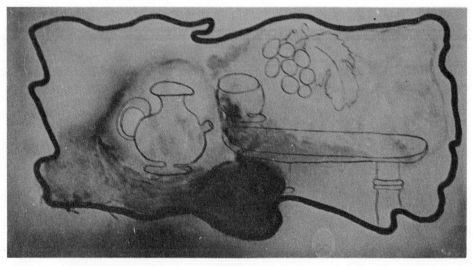

Painting by Diulgheroff for the quisibeve at the Holy Palate Restaurant.

little
dictionary of
futurist cooking

castagne candite:
replaces **marrons glacés**

conprofumo:
term that indicates the olfactory affinity of a given perfume with the flavour of a given food. Example: the *conprofumo* of pulped potato and roses.

contattile:
term that indicates the tactile affinity of a given material with the flavour of a given food. Example: the *contattile* of banana and velvet, or female flesh.

conrumore:
term that indicates the sound affinity of a given noise with the flavour of a given food. Example: the *conrumore* of rice in orange sauce and a motorcycle engine, or 'The Awakening of the City' by the Futurist *rumorist* Luigi Russolo.

conmusica:
term that indicates the acoustic affinity of a given piece of music with the flavour of a given food. Example: the *conmusica* of the Sculpted Meat and the ballet 'HOP-FROG' by the Futurist maestro Franco Casavola.

conluce:
term that indicates the optical affinity of a given light with the flavour of a given food. Example: the *conluce* of the 'Excited Pig' and a streak of red lightning.

consumato:
replaces **consommé.**

decisone:

generic name for hot-tonic *polibibite* that help one to make after a short but profound meditation, an important decision.

disprofumo:

term that indicates the complementary nature of a given perfume with the flavour of a given food. Example: the *disprofumo* of raw meat and jasmine.

distattile:

term that indicates the complementary nature of a given material with the flavour of a given food. Example: the *distattile* of the 'Equator + North Pole' and a sponge.

disrumore:

term that indicates the complementary nature of a given sound with the flavour of a given food. Example: the *disrumore* of the 'Italian Sea' and the hiss of hot oil, bubbly drinks and sea foam.

dismusica:

term that indicates the complementary nature of a given piece of music with the flavour of a given food. Example: the *dismusica* of dates with anchovies and Beethoven's Ninth Symphony.

disluce:

term that indicates the complementary nature of a given light with the flavour of a given food. Example: the *disluce* of chocolate ice-cream and a hot orange light.

fondenti:

replaces **fondants.**

fumatoio:
replaces **fumoir.**

guerrainletto:
a fertilizing *polibibita.*

inventina:
generic name for refreshing and slightly inebriating *polibibite* that help one to find a new idea suddenly.

lista or listavivande:
replaces **menu.**

mescitore:
replaces **barman.**

miscela:
replaces **mélange.**

paceinletto:
soporific *polibibita.*

pasticcio:
replaces **flan.**

peralzarsi:
replaces **dessert.**

polibibita:
replaces **cocktail.**

poltiglia:
replaces **purée.**

pranzoalsole:
replaces **picnic.**

prestoinletto:
warming winter *polibibita*.

quisibeve:
replaces **bar.**

sala da té:
replaces **tea-room.**

sganasciatore:
Futurist personality whose job it is to enliven official banquets.

traidue:
replaces **sandwich**

zuppa di pesce:
replaces **bouillabaisse.**